THE DARK

Of An Animal Farmer

A true story of one man's dark experiences as an animal farmer, and the events that led to his transformation into an animal defender.

A note from the editor:

In 'The Dark Secrets of an Animal Farmer, Mark Moore courageously exposes the concealed realities behind the picturesque facade of the farming industry. Once a farmer deeply entrenched in this world, Mark transforms into a dedicated vegan advocate, unravelling a compelling narrative that unveils the hidden truths of modern agriculture.

As an insider turned whistleblower, I found Mark's story to be inspiring as his unwavering honesty provides an unfiltered glimpse into the practices of contemporary farming, shedding a light on the sacrifices made by both animals, and farmers. This tale exposes the relentless pursuit of profit, and the dark compromises that are necessary to sustain it.

This story however, transcends despair, offering a tale of both transformation, and redemption. Mark undergoes a profound awakening to the ethical implications of his previous actions, both the ones that he chose of his own free will, and the ones imposed upon him since childhood.

This book has not only the potential, but the power, to cause you as the reader to reconsider your own role in the intricate web of the food industry.

WARNING: This book contains graphic descriptions of animal cruelty and violence that some readers may find distressing, mentions of severe mental health repercussions, and suicide. Please read on at your own discretion.

I am no man, nor am I a woman.

I am not a child of gender.

I will have no value to you.

I cannot be boxed, bottled, nor sold.

I am but a faint voice carried on the winds of change.

I do not exist until I am heard.

I cannot hear until my works are read.

I belonged to a time that was long past, a time that will not resurrect.

Read on… and we will be acquainted.

INTRODUCTION

I look at the dark silhouette of the old farm. It lies empty, almost derelict. It seems at peace now. The shouting and swearing are gone. The cries of the animals disappeared in the same wind that twisted and shaped the old cherry tree that stands beside it. Like all old places it has secrets, but some secrets are better left untold and let die with their keepers. Others, however, must be told; for they are destined to become a story. Maybe a story that will bring the winds of change to this world.

I am going to tell you that story. It's the story of my life. But if it was just the story of my life then believe me, I surely would not tell it. This story is of farm animals. Not just any farm animals, but the animals that have shared my life. But be warned, there is no joy to be found in this tale. No tears of happiness, no heartwarming ending. There is pain and suffering, heartbreak and sadness.

However, take courage; there is hope to be found within these pages. Not a fool's hope, but a powerful hope; the kind that can lift the spirits of the oppressed to rise from their chains and strike down their cruel masters.

Though at times the story is dark and difficult, there is love to be found in this recollection. The kind of love that you would find in a good romance novella, also, just a touch of humour. The dark times have shaped the days that I live today. The coldness and hardness of my heart I will use as my strength, as I endeavor to bring change for farm animals everywhere. These cruel memories that distorted my perception of life and shaped me into a hard person, I can only hope will awaken the kindness in the heart of whoever reads them. I have lived many years without meat and dairy. Maybe you will too.

This is not for me, but for those without choice, those who suffer voiceless and hopeless now and the ghosts of yesterday. For those keep me from my sleep at night. I see the ghosts that hinder my peace of mind, yet I dare not hold communion with them. I would feel ridiculous to trust anything they could say, for their world and mine should never meet on equal terms; and neither one could comprehend each others existence. It is better to render one's senses corrupt, than wear such nonsense on your lips.

I am not so young as, nor yet of an old enough age, where nonsense is acceptable. Once given the denomination of madman it is yours for life. So read on with the confidence that nothing is presumed or channeled from beyond. I have experienced it all through my worldly senses. Take solace in the knowledge that even a hardened animal abuser like myself can change to become an animal defender.

This is a story of farm animal abuse. It should be taken as an act of activism. It is intended to bring change.

Like all, I have known hard times and I have known them easy. I have travelled the path that has been laid before me and stumbled and fallen from time to time. My upbringing has forced me to take part in some horrific acts of animal cruelty, and for this I will always be ashamed. It has been said however, that every cloud, no matter how dark and enraged, has a silver lining. I hope that this book will be the one modicum of good that can come from the tragedies that I have witnessed and participated in. I hope to provide an insight into the mentality of the farming community, and the heavy conditioning that people are raised with. One which convinces them that living beings are mere products of their industry; revealing the mental strain that it can cause on the people who make a career out of murder and abuse.

When I finally adopted veganism as a cornerstone in my life, I was forced to turn my back on my kind. On family and friends who refused to understand my choices; on a way of life that had been mine for over a quarter of a century. A lifestyle passed down through generations was lost to me. When it was gone I waited for a sense of grief to consume me, due to being deprived of a community that I had known for my whole life. To my surprise, that grief never came. I lost my people when I turned vegan, and all I could feel was an overwhelming sense of enlightenment. I slowly began to realise that those who had turned their backs on me were not my people at all, and they never had been. Take solace in the knowledge that even a hardened animal abuser like me can change to become an animal defender.

I am no longer a part of the farming community. I am a vegan, and I am **proud**.

CHAPTER ONE:
THE YEARS THAT
SHAPED ME

I look at the dark silhouette of the old farm. It lies empty, almost derelict. The rage filled shouting, the profanities hurled like stones that bruised the innocence of my young soul, the sense of dread that hung in the frosty air, they're all gone now. The cries of the animals disappeared in the same wind that twisted and shaped the old cherry tree that stands beside it. The land seems at peace. It's bittersweet to see the natural wildlife returning to the surrounding fields, the wire cages that once entrapped one species of bird are now opened and willingly a home to another species. Their little nests, delicately woven out of branches and leaves that have fallen from the trees that I used to climb in my youth give me a sense of wonder that reminds me that even though we are all different species, we are all still part of the greater ecosystem of this planet.

The mother mouse that huddles for warmth under an old grain sack in the barn to shelter her young is not so different from myself as I stack logs onto my open fire to keep my own children warm. It seems so obvious to me now as I watch nature beginning to reclaim this once rigid farmland, that this is how the land is supposed to be. Gentle. Kind. A place for life to thrive. How did I not see it before? How did my parents not see it? And their parents before them? I wish that my childhood has been filled with memories just like this one, but unfortunately, that was not the case.

A frozen heart beats cold,

It speaks cold words and performs cold deeds.

The hatred of a frozen heart freezes all who it touches.

Your icy grip I still feel around my heart.

I was born on a farm in Lancashire, a beautiful county in the North of England. Its business was mostly centred around cattle, providing dairy and beef to the surrounding community. We did however also deal in sheep, horses and poultry. The building itself was a 16th century farmhouse with old oak beams, stone flag floors, and magnificent views north across the Yorkshire border to the dales. It had old barns and buildings filled with horses, cows, sheep, hens and occasionally even a pig or two. A traveller passing by the farm once told me that I was born with a silver spoon in my mouth to live in such a beautiful place; in many ways he was right.

I loved the beautiful countryside and I lived by and the wildlife that I shared it with. You will find, however, that not every silver spoon is loaded with sugar, some are heaped with a generous helping of salt. This farm was a place of fear, pain and suffering. My earliest memory from childhood was not a happy one.

I have three older sisters. One that is ten years my elder and I will say to her credit that I have had no reason to complain about her. Two of the sisters however, are twins, and they are six years older than me. I hold no deep affection for them, and in turn they would rather have me as a memorial in the cemetery than aspire to be above them. Jealousy, greed, lies and deception have taken their heart and they revel in their disposition. They carry the cross of Jesus in one hand and the holy lance in the other, while spitting venom at all who make kindness their business.

I clearly remember the twins taking me down the grassy fields by the side of the Leeds/Liverpool canal. One sister pushed me to the ground and told me that my mother and father did not love me and that they only had me so I could work on the farm when I got older.

Her eyes were wild and she looked almost excited, as if she genuinely enjoyed causing me emotional distress. (This is a trait that over time has been shown to be recurring.) She then grabbed my hair and swung me around and beat me. I remember seeing my blond curly hair in her hands as it ripped from my head, and feeling the burning sting that it left behind. She put her hand over my mouth roughly, and told me to shut up or I would get more.

They would then both then abandon me, crying, scared and alone near the canal. I was four years old, and I didn't know my way back.

Eventually they would come back and cuddle me, wrapping me up in a hug that felt devoid of any real warmth or love, but nonetheless was still comforting. I felt instant relief as they kissed me better and told me they were sorry, but the apologies lacked any real sincerity, and this scenario happened over and over. As the months and years went by and I grew weary of their attention. If I could remember one good deed they have done for anyone, then I would relate it.

The kinder of the two twins made me two stuffed toy cats that she named big cat and little cat. I loved them. She would come into my room and make them talk to me, I still remember to this day the warmth I felt when I saw them, although this feeling didn't last. She would make them die, and consequently, make me cry. When she thought I was sad enough she would resurrect them in an attempt to cheer me up, but by this point the damage was done. If I mention this today she just laughs and tells me not to be so soft. I never told my parents about this, as I thought this was just normal behaviour until years later when I told my wife about it and saw the shock on her face.

The more mean of the two twins was much worse. She would keep on with her incessant bullying until I was about eleven years old, she would be about seventeen then. She was violent and cruel, and her actions wore me down until one day I couldn't take it any longer and I retaliated. She slapped me in the face when we were preparing to milk the cows, and as I felt the warm sting of pain on my cheek the tension that had been building within me over the years began to rise to a dangerous level. I'm not proud of what I did next, nor do I regret it. To put things bluntly, I attacked her. I violently kicked her in her head after punching her to the ground, letting out every ounce of rage, every modicum of resentment, until there was nothing left within me and I felt calm again.

From that day, to this, she switched to mental abuse. I was too physically strong.

Although I had managed to spare myself any more beatings from my terrible sister, I did receive quite a scolding from my father, who did not like me hitting a girl no matter the age difference between us, or the actions that had caused it. After a long day of work I was sent straight to bed and was left in my small dreary bedroom to contemplate my actions. Things often happen for a reason and on that stormy night in my bedroom I wrote my first poem. I wrote it on the back cover of my 1977 Brere Rabbit Annual. I recently found the book and rediscovered this poem after my mother's death. It went like this:

The Hermit

One stormy night as I lay awake and the weather

played my window pain, What a lonely tune the wind

whistled out to the beat drummed by the rain.
And the groan of beams in this tired old house
gave words to the dreary old song,

And I rose from my bed and I started to dance, I
was naked but it didn't feel wrong.

Then an owls did screech from the limb of a tree which was strange for
such a stormy old night,
And the clouds came apart for a second or two and the room filled
with bright moonlight.

It was then that I saw that I wasn't alone, a
shadow had took up the dance,

And though I only saw him for that second or two I was glad that I
caught him in a glance.

Then the moon came back out and we dance through

> *the night to music of this terrible*
> *band,*

> *The shadow and I danced a right merry jig, I*
> *tell you, the feeling was grand.*

> *We dance all the night, till the dawn crept in and my shadow friend*
> *must of gone home to bed,*
> *And I sat on my chair at the back of the room and thought, " did that*
> *happen or was it all in my head"?*

Looking back, I guess I was always a little strange, or at the very least I didn't quite fit in with the company that I was made to keep, but I remember writing the poem and feeling very proud. Despite my pride, I never did show it to my family though. There was no point. They were more interested in how hard I could work than whether or not I could make a satisfying rhyme, or create a compelling story. It's a shame to think back on, and I often wonder what would have become of my life if I had been able to nurture my passion for creativity, writing, and art, rather than having to work on that farm for hours on end every day.

Another integral part of my childhood was a time that I less than tenderly refer to as 'The Big Depression'. This is what I call the five or so years that my father became depressed. He would have violent temper tantrums, constantly singing songs made up in their entirety from swear words. Almost every milking time he would be kicking and shouting at the cows, an action that happened often enough to completely desensitise me from the concept of casual animal cruelty from a young age.

Believe it or not, I only remember my father hitting me once. This was when I was around four years old. He rented a farm nearby, and needed to move some cows from the field where they grazed into a building where they could be kept warm. He told me, a child not yet old enough or tall enough to even see into the bathroom mirror, to stand in the track to stop the stampeding herd of cows from running onto the road. Without question, I stood there at about three feet tall, and waited bravely. Soon enough the cows came running towards me at high speed, the sound of their hooves growing louder as they moved from grass to gravel, and I jumped up and down and shouted in an attempt to stop them. I tried with all of my might, but they weren't stopping. In a state of panic, I finally lost my nerve and dove out of the way, leaving the cows to run onto the country road. My Dad hit the roof, he shouted at me and kicked me hard in my bottom. I still remember the pain as I was left at the side of the track crying while he set off after the cows. To his credit, when I confronted him about this over twenty years later he did admit that he was very sorry. To be honest, I had already forgiven him. I knew how much extra work I caused him by stepping out of the way.

When my father was deep in his depression, he would very rarely, if at all, speak to any of us. He would bark orders at us, of course, and he would shout and swear and be constantly angry. The thing that confused me most however, was that if his friends called round to visit, he would be perfectly normal. He would laugh and joke and be an extremely happy person, as if all of the stress had been lifted off his shoulders within that moment. I talked to my mother about it years later, and she said he had been to the doctor for help but they said he needed to 'snap out of it'. Of course, mental health wasn't taken as seriously back then as it should have been. To this day, I still don't believe that it is.

My mother was scared that my father was going to hang himself at that time, as he had told her he wanted to. At the time she didn't understand what he was going through, and neither did I... Well, not yet anyway.

I expect that there will be those of you that feel a little sorry for young infant Mark, but I urge you: Do not. I became hardened and cruel from the experiences of my childhood years. I fought and bullied people at school. In fact, I fought so much in my first ten years of life that I didn't need to fight at all when I went to high school. I had gained a less than stellar reputation, and people simply knew to keep out of my way.

There were about five other farmer's children in my year at school, and they were all so radiantly proud of being brought up on a farm. They would all sit together, telling tales of their work and the industry in which they were raised. In fact, they would bring farming up at any chance they would get. Personally, I just didn't get it. I could never understand why I wasn't proud of being the son of an animal farmer like they were, why when they spoke out about their upbringing I tended to shy away and bow my head into my desk. I hated it. I felt like I was inferior, like I smelled bad, and in turn I became a terribly shy teenager. I couldn't speak out in class without going very red in the face, and this made the whole class laugh every time I was called upon to do so. I think the shyness was a result of my fathers strict and fiercely guarded rules. I couldn't speak unless spoken to. I had to address adults as Mr or Mrs or Miss, followed by their surname. I had to ask permission to leave the table and we had endless chores to do. School break was a time of constant work for me, as it was for many farmer's sons, but where others seemed to find fulfilment, I despised doing it. Perhaps I was always destined to become a vegan, not that I could've ever even fathomed the concept back then.

I understand that my childhood was not the most traumatising, and was nowhere near as terrible as some of the tales that I have heard from others. We always had food, clothing, and moderate wealth. We worked backbreaking hours on that farm in the rain and the snow and the frost, but in a way we were lucky to at least have enough work to get by as a family. My youth, however, was very different to that of the children who were allowed to sleep in on the weekends, who were allowed to play outside with their friends, to sit for hours in front of the television, and who could speak to their parents about their issues and receive nothing but love in return. When I look back at the experiences that shaped me, I can almost see why I ended up as the cold, animal abuser that I did for so many years.

CHAPTER 2: HORSES

Not so fun fact: horses are still consumed by humans in the UK. There are three abattoirs in the UK licensed to slaughter horses for human consumption. Horses are usually killed by a free bullet into their brain, then they are shackled by their hind legs, raised, and their throats are cut to bleed them out. Most UK horses end their lives being slaughtered for consumption.

Throughout my years as a farmer's son, and a farmer, we farmed cows, pigs, sheep and hens, and we also dealt in horses. These horses however, were not a matter of pounds and pence to me as the others once were; they were more like beloved pets. It was actually a horse that changed my life, that planted the seed of kindness in my heart that eventually bloomed and opened my eyes to the possibility that all animals love and want to be loved in return.

A Meditation

The fences will fall and will open up to an endless sky.

Yet there is a darker sky in you than the portraits that you paint; though it is hidden and will

not be revealed.

You lust for something more, something stronger than you already have. As it slowly

begins to emerge you feel its pull.

Is that a light that you see at the end of the tunnel or just a speck of white paint on the

eternal black canvas.

Madness would take you if not for that thought; and it keeps you, as you keep it. Reach out and accept what your heart desires and the new clean air will fill your lungs and the vastness of possibilities will be your future.

Let go of the rocks that drags you downwards and you will float to the surface and breathe again.

The food is yours to eat or yours to leave and it's nourishment is abstract. From the beginning to the end, your life is the milk of the breast and revels in the pleasures of serenity.

Tomorrow the sun will shine and all storms avail, to reveal a landscape long masked from you. Is it better to see the beauty of the apple blossom sky than to follow the casket? Dim your expectations and you will see more beauty than could ever be promised; feel more love than could ever be foretold and all desires quenched.

If you are falling then just reach out your hand and you will be upheld.

If you are burning then trust the cool waters are there to cool you.

Above all things look no further than your pocket, for what you seek is not lost. The crispness of a frosty day will reveal the path and it must be followed. A woodland cottage once alive with flowers is now subdued by winter's chill. The wisteria, though lost and shrivelled, is no more gone than spring is lost forever. It is the way of life that all things live forever.

There cannot be another way.

Though I have had the great fortune of spending time with many horses, I am going to tell you of one particular horse that became my companion and friend through some of my darkest times. Horses were, and will always be a great love of mine. It was once my job to break them, groom them and shoe them. I had a calm, quiet way with the horses and was known in family circles as a whisperer.

I have travelled the country roads around Yorkshire and Cumbria with my horses and spent happy times with my wife Louise and my beautiful children. We met many Gypsies and travellers, companions and friends who became strong acquaintances over the years. Many times I have heard derogatory stories about the travelling community and I would like to set the record straight. I have never met a group of people who have such high moral standards, nor met anybody who cared more for their animals as the Gypsies and travellers that I have shared time with. If the farming industry treated their animals one third as well as these people then I would have no need to write this book. That's all I will say about that, as their story is not mine to tell.

I will tell you the story of my friend Dobby.

Dobby was a black yearling gelding when I bought him from an auction in Ilkley. He had three white socks that hung over his hooves, and a small white star on his forehead. He was about thirteen hands high, fifteen by the time he had reached the age of five, and he had a soft, gentle temperament. Dobby was born in 2002, and my daughters named him Dobby after the house elf from the Harry Potter books. From the very start he loved the attention. He loved my daughters grooming him and petting him, feeding him and talking to him. My father would tell me off about this at times,

" You'll bloody spoil yon hoss treating it like a pet," he would scold.

My father was loud around horses, he always had been, and in turn they were always a little jumpy when he was near. He was the sort of man who would try and force a horse to do what he wanted. Anybody who truly knows horses will know that a horse only has to understand what it is that you would like them to do and then they will quickly try to please. Fear has no place in training a horse. Quiet kindness will be quickly repaid with forbearance, for restraint, control, and tolerance are the qualities of a horse, and without them we would have no sway over their actions whatsoever.

Dobby showed great tolerance to me and my children and I endeavoured to repay him with as much kindness as was in me at that time. I would bring him from the field at around 5.30am and take him out around the winding roads, revelling in the golden glow of the sunrise as Dobby pulled the exercise cart before returning to the farm. His hooves would pound against the hard stone of the farmyard ground, and I would stop Dobby by the side of his barn, un-harness him, and groom him.. At that time I had taken to wearing a hat, my hair was receding and I felt a little self-conscious about it. Dobby, knowing that directly after the grooming he would have a bucket of bran for his breakfast, would grab my hat with his mouth and throw it on the floor. This happened every morning and it never sped up the grooming; it only succeeded in prolonging the process.

While he was eating I would leave him in the yard and then go to the old farmhouse and chat to my father. Soon enough I would hear his hooves on the stone flags outside and then he would press his nose to the window. My mother would get in a flap about her clean windows being dirtied by that silly horse and I would be sent out to remove him, a smile on my face each and every time. I would then open the gate to the fields and he would spend his day eating and basking in the sunshine, or sheltering from the rain under the many low hanging trees. At this point in my life I was going through a divorce with my first wife and a harsh depression had taken me. I truly think that I might have taken my own life if it was not for Dobby and of course my good friend John, a good kind man who has no place in this book of horrors. If not for him and Dobby I would not be here.

At the end of May, Myself, my wife, and my children would set off on the eighty mile journey to Appleby, a small town in Westmorland. Every year in early June the town would hold a huge horse fair, and people would travel from all over the country with their families and their horses and their friends to join the merriments. Dobby and another horse would pull the BowTop caravan down the country roads, through quaint villages and towns and occasionally past busier areas where people would stop and watch us go by. I would often walk by his side. We would take a full two weeks to travel to the fair and we would only cover about 5 miles in a single day. We would stop for the night in fields by the side of country roads and camp under the moonlight, and sometimes I would lay up at night with Dobby to watch the stars. It was a magical time for our family, one that we all still talk about with a great fondness.

Once we finally arrived at the crowded fair, my feet blistered from the walking, Dobby would love the attention of the crowds. His ears would perk up when he heard the strange noises, and his head would turn when he smelled the scent of the street food. I have, however, taken other horses who were not so happy there, so it was just Dobby's thing I suppose. He seemed to enjoy his time in Appleby so much that he knew when the time had come to an end, and he was due to set off back home. He would quicken his steps and be restless at each camp on the journey back, and when we made it home in around five days time his work was done for that year. Why I cared so much for a horse and so little for other farm animals I will never understand. I can only liken it to people loving a dog but eating a pig. There is no sense in it.

One hot summer's day I had brought Dobby in from the sun and tied him in a building, as I so often did when I needed to keep him safe and contained for a little while. I had put his tether collar on, clipped it to a round-hank on the concrete boskin, and left him with a bucket of grain. Two traveller friends of mine had called and I was chatting to them in the yard, content and calm in the warm sunlight and happy in good company. I could hear Dobby tapping his feet in the building, itching them as he often did, I thought. I carried on talking and laughing with my friends, maying the sound of his hooves no mind, when I suddenly began to realise that the tapping of feet began to sound... different somehow. This wasn't the norm, and although I was sure that it may have been nothing, I excused myself from my friends and went to see what was going on.

The sight that greeted me sent me into panic.

He had somehow gotten his head over the concrete boskin and he was strangeling. Desperate, I darted to his side and tried to loosen the collar, but it was too tight around his neck. I could feel my heart begin to pound, and a cold sensation overtook my body as I realised that there was nothing I could do in this moment to help him, not on my own anyway. I ran out to my friends, shouting something I can barely remember and before I knew what was happening one of them had handed me a knife. I ran in and cut the leather collar with such speed that I would have marvelled in any other circumstance.

The collar was freed, but Dobby lay lifeless on the ground. Not quite knowing what to do next, I threw myself against his body with my full weight, over and over, trying urgently to get his heart beating again, or air back in his lungs. I tried so hard and for so long that by the time it was over I was drenched with sweat. My friends had to drag me out. "He's gone, " they said, holding me back. I calmed quickly and regained my composure, trying my best to be aware of my surroundings as my head was dizzy, and my ears were ringing. My friends looked pale, baffled by what had happened, possibly even shocked with how they had seen me react. They asked me if I was ok. I nodded 'yes,' a lie, and said, these things happen. They shook my hand and left.

Once everybody had left, there was only myself, and the deafening silence.

I calmly walked back into my old friend and dropped down beside his lifeless body. The tears began to form in the corners of my eyes, and before I knew it I was weeping and crying out that I was sorry. A full hour I stayed with him pleading for him to revive, hoping that he was only unconscious. But really I knew, for I am sure I felt his faint heartbeat stop and felt him draw his last breath before his collar was cut.

I returned home to break the news to my poor wife Louise and my beautiful children. It wasn't a pleasant conversation to say the least, but I never let the children know exactly how Dobby had passed. Dobby had helped me through the worst of my depression, he was there when I remarried under the bridge at Clapham on our annual journey to Appleby horse fair. He was a true friend who I miss to this day and will miss until my last. I am forever sorry for my carelessness. Never again will I ask an animal to work for me, because most who do, never wait for an answer.

I have one more story to tell you about Dobby. It's a story that gives me peace and hope for my old friend. I know that ghosts have walked the house, buildings and yard of this farm. I have seen them as clear as my own reflection in the mirror; so I don't find this tale as unbelievable as you might.

Dobby and I were known for taking the dead on their final journey to the church if the deceased had requested a horse-drawn funeral. So I wasn't too surprised to get a call from a man from the Barrow-in-Furness area. If I recall correctly his name was Tony. If I am wrong I apologise, but he will be called Tony herewith. His mother was terminally ill and her final wish was to have a ride in a horse drawn caravan, the way that she had seen the travellers do it, a real adventure in her eyes. It was something that she had always wanted, something she told me was on her 'bucket list'. After a very interesting conversation with Tony we agreed to do the trip, however the night before we were due to travel up to Barrow, my truck's water pump broke and had no replacement for a few days. I called Tony and explained what had happened, and requested that we postpone the trip.

I could tell though, that this was going to be a source of great disappointment for Tony, and for his mother as well. It couldn't be easy having a relative with a terminal illness, the pressure to fulfil their final wishes, the thought of how little time you may have to make these dreams happen. I knew that no matter what, we had to find a way to make this work.

With great difficulty I spent my day making phone calls until finally, I managed to borrow a truck, and the job was back on.

It was a warm morning when we arrived. I met the family and the terminally ill woman. She seemed kind and happy, still so full of life. I knew that this would be one of her final memories before she was taken from this world, so it had to go perfectly. We harnessed Dobby into the shafts of the gypsy caravan and after petting Dobby and getting to know him Tony's mother climbed aboard the vardo. Dobby seemed very happy with her, and reacted differently than he did with most strangers. This was unusual behaviour indeed from my old horse. He would normally throw his head about and fidget when a stranger petted him. It seemed that the two of them had an instant connection.When you know someone so well, you can see little reactions that only you will notice; and Dobby really liked this particular lady.

The family had mapped a route of about 5 or 6 miles of quiet countryside and we rambled along in the warm sunshine. The lady chatted happily all the way round. She told me about the red soil up there, talked of local families and the history of the area. Then, quite out of the blue, she announced to Dobby that she was going to steal him from me and that they were going to go on an adventure together. I thought nothing about this statement. I politely laughed and said, " You would like that wouldn't you Dob?" We carried on our way and returned to the large crowd of family members.

Later that evening we returned home and went about our lives until a month or two later, when Dobby tragically passed away. It was only two days after, that I received a call from Tony. He told me that his mother had passed away too. He told us that she had loved the trip, and had talked about it in her final hour. She had died on the same day that Dobby had. Tony had taken some of Dobby's hair and was going to put it in the coffin with his mother. With the ashes he was going to have a tattoo of Dobby and the vardo to remember his mother by. To me she had kept her word. She had stolen Dobby from me and they were off on their adventures together. They are out there still, rambling the roads and byways of that red soiled country that she loved so much.

CHAPTER 3: THE ESCAPE

A godless villain seeks riches buried on distant shores.

But his treasure lies beneath the feet of his kin.

So deeply did Dobby's death cut me that I became withdrawn to the world. For the whole of the autumn and winter I performed my duties on auto-pilot.

My wife and I owned a cafe in the village at this time, and I had a flock of sheep that I tended with all that I had left to give. I feel deep regret on how I treated my beautiful, kind wife and my enduring children. I forgot to eat food and lived mainly on water for a while. I would take a drop or two of wormwood oil as a precaution against internal parasites. I had seen what these parasites could do to a sheep and I didn't wish this for myself.

One day in early December, all feelings of duty and honour left me. I had felt numb for such a long time, trudging through my daily life with very little feeling other than discontent, and melancholy.

I packed a bag and walked out on my life, not recognising it as mine anymore. Without a second thought, I threw my phone into a hedgerow of bare hawthorn, and headed for god knows where, for I was trusting him to guide me. As I wandered over the moors above the quaint Yorkshire town of Skipton, my inflicted and paranoid mind made me feel as though I must be being hunted by my family or the police, so I skulked in the shadows; concealed by the tall drystone walls and twisted grasping trees, silhouetted by a fading sky. Night had caught up to me and though I preferred its company to the revealing daylight, it made it almost impossible to walk through the soaking heather and peaty bogs. In the near distance I could just make out the shape of a building. When I approached it I could see it was an old out-barn with an open door. I entered it, hoping to seek shelter from the now biting wind. I could see that cows had recently used it for their shelter too. It was deep in mud and excrement, but I found the driest corner and laid down my weary body. There were sounds of rustling and squeaking as I lay awake, numb to my sane mind and spurred on by a false sense of god's will.

Somewhere in the darkness I must have passed into sleep, because I woke to the sound of a quad bike in the distance. I gathered my things and like a fox, slipped unnoticed into the countryside. Before long I came to the road that led either south to Colne or North to Skipton. My heart had always preferred to head north so I followed the road to Skipton. At the side of the road after walking about two miles I found a stout stick, I examined it and recognised it as being cut from a hazel tree. This would be my companion for a while. I entered Skipton and after receiving some peculiar looks and a cheeky remark from some school children I realised that I must have looked like an odd sort of fellow. I was mud stained and bedraggled, and walking with a large pack on my back and my hazel staff I understood the comment made by the young, wood-be scrollers. "All right Mr Frodo, heading to mount doom are you?" I chuckled to myself and appreciated the witty humour.

After a trip into the local Tesco for supplies that I bought using money that I had obtained by selling my horse drawn caravan a few days earlier, I sat outside the train station and drank a bottle of water. The walk had made me thirsty, and a warm sun had made me sweat. A couple walked past me and were chatting excitedly about the trip they were taking on the Settle-Carlisle railway. They seemed oblivious to my presence on the bench.
I took this as a sign from god, and decided to go on the same trip myself.

" You better run, sir, it's due to leave any minute."

The assistant told me as I hurriedly paid for my ticket. I ran as fast as I could with a large bag and a now cumbersome staff, and made it with mere seconds to spare. The nicest seat that was free was the one by the window, facing forward on the left hand side of the train. What a beautiful journey it was. We passed through pretty villages and over viaducts. Over moors and through sunlight valleys with meandering rivers. The sudden injection of darkness into my otherwise bright journey as we shot through long dark tunnels filled my heart with joy, and I felt like god was indeed plotting my adventure.

Eventually, I pulled into Carlisle station, and was greeted by a billboard advertising the bustling Scottish city of Edinburgh. Without delay I then bought a ticket to Waverley Station. Again the train was due to leave immediately. I ran to the platform and was ushered onto the train by two attendants, who seemed pleasantly amused by the rough appearance. I found a seat and the train sped out of Carlisle. After a while a gentleman with a trolly offered me a cup of tea and a biscuit. I politely accepted and enjoyed both. It was the first food that I had consumed for days and it must have awakened me a little to reality. I thought of my wife and family and my heart was nipped with the pinch of guilt's grip.

God knows what he is doing, I thought. It's funny how we can use God to excuse our selfish behaviour.

My guilt was interrupted by the conductor asking for my ticket. I handed it to him and after studying it he asked me if I would like to upgrade to first class. I smiled and told him no and that I was happy here thanks. He laughed and explained that I was in fact already sitting in First class, and that I would have to move to coach or pay the difference. I wasn't accustomed to train travel so had no idea. Without a word, I moved to the next coach and continued my journey. It turned out that there was only about ten minutes of the journey left and I felt that God had looked after me quite well. Waverly Station was busy when I finally arrived. There were so many different people around, and I wove my way between them with my staff strapped to the side of my backpack. My clothes were dirty and I probably still had the aroma of the cow shed that I had slept in the night before. I had been to Edinburgh once before and I remembered my way around the centre, so I decided to make my way up to the castle.

The town was busy with tourists and I could tell that my hobbit-like appearance was quite amusing to some of them. A family speaking a language I didn't understand, quite obviously tourists, actually stopped and asked for a photo with me. I obliged and afterwards they offered me a £5.00 note. I accepted gratefully and continued up the royal mile. The air carried the sound of merry bagpipes playing through the streets, past street performers and singers, and a lady with piercings on every part of her body who saw herself as some sort of attraction. Well, I think every part, at least that's what her billboard said. There was even a very convincing William Wallace from the "BraveHeart" film. He smiled and nodded at me as I went past.

A charitable feeling came upon me and I handed him the £5.00 note that was still crumpled up in my hand. He took it and smiled again, but neither of us said a word. Weary from my walk, I sat on the floor and leaned against the wall in the large courtyard at the top of the Royal Mile. I had grown increasingly tired from my journey, and I thought about where I would stay. Another man took a photo of me as I sat there and I realised that it was my staff strapped to the side of my backpack that looked unusual. I supposed it gave off a romantic image of an old-world tinker or traveller. I removed the staff and laid it down by the side of the wall. That's where my companion and I parted, and spent the next few hours wandering around the city in search of a sign that would reveal the next part of my journey to me.

I ended up walking for longer than I had hoped, and before too long I had earned myself a pretty painful blister on my right heel. Restless, I peered into shop windows, gazing into one in particular that was advertising trips to the Isle of Skye. I thought that I would like to take that trip. I had a little less than £800.00 in my pocket from the sale of the caravan, so I was feeling quite flush. Looking back now I feel selfish. I had seven children and a wife at home, and we were always short on money. What was I thinking?

I will chalk it down to God's will and excuse myself for now. I don't have time for self-loathing; I have a story to tell.

Luckily the next shop down the street had a sign that told me that for only £12.00 per night I could have a bed. I suppose that meant I now had some semblance of a home for the night. I would be sharing a room with nine other people, all much younger than me, and most of them foreign travellers. Upon entering the dorm I realised my own aroma and felt a little self conscious. A young man who later I learned was from Spain went and opened a window. I needed a wash and that was for sure. After unpacking I went into the shower room, noticing some shower gel on the windowsill. I was well aware that this belonged to one of the other hostel guests, however, I am sorry to say that I used it anyway, tried myself on one of their towels, even stole a pea sized blob of toothpaste that I rubbed onto my teeth with my bare finger. I was too tired, too dizzy from the lack of food, and too in need of a real wash to care much. The moment my head hit the pillow that night, I was out like a light.

It was a pleasant surprise that breakfast was included in the £12.00 I paid for the bed, but you had to make it yourself. I could have cereal and two slices of toast. If you remember, I had eaten nothing for days with the exception of the biscuit on the train; so I buttered two slices of toast and had some muesli with milk. I took the toast back to my room and put it into my locker for my evening meal.

I was still unsure of my purpose here, but I knew that I needed to do something so I decided to look for work. I walked from pub to pub, cafe to cafe, enquiring if they needed help. I had been a cook in the cafe for a couple of years and I was pretty good under pressure. Nearly all of them asked for a contact number, but I didn't have a phone anymore.

I returned to my hostel and wandered up to my dorm. At first glance it seemed empty so I laid on my bed and let my mind wander. I think the breakfast must have been reviving my brain because guilt started to enter it and I missed my family. These thoughts however, were interrupted by the sound of a girl crying. I listened for a while, unsure of what I should do, before I decided to peer round the corner of a bunk bed to see a young girl, easily only in her very early twenties, sobbing bitterly on her bed. I sat on the bottom bunk of my bed, smiled, and asked if she was alright. She looked up at me. She didn't seem surprised to see me so I presume she must have heard me enter the dorms. I have never been accused of being light footed, so it made sense. The girl was eager to tell me that she was homesick. She had left Australia the previous January and travelled Europe. She had come to Edinburgh two months earlier and had found it more difficult to find friends. The girl just wanted to go home but she was booked on a flight at the end of January and it was only December. She said that she was going to ask her parents for money to get a sooner flight, and she told me this through bitter tears.

Now, it turns out that I was quite good at motivating people, and straight away I fell into a speech of some sort. It went like this:

"Have you ever read the novel "The Hobbit?"

I asked. I suppose that idea came from the cheeky young boy who called me Mr Frodo, back in Skipton. She answered yes. I went on to explain how almost all of the adventure that Bilbo experienced, he missed his home comforts and more than once he wanted to leave and go back home.

"He didn't though," I smiled.

"He carried on and his adventures continued."

If we move forward to The Lord Of The Rings, Bilbo is sat with his family, happily telling tales of his adventures to Rivendell and The Lonely Mountain . He tells tales of his encounters with trolls and the friendships that he made. How he longs to go back one day, I explained. The girl gave me her full attention now.

"That is you young lady,"

I told her. "One day you will be old and telling your grandchildren about your adventures through Europe. And although Edinburgh is the hardest part, you will speak of it more fondly than any other. Don't go home early. Instead make it an adventure worthy of telling your grandchildren."

I think the tears that I saw reappearing in her eyes were tears of motivation. She made a special effort to find me the next day and proudly told me she had booked a trip to the Isle of Skye and was going to stay in Edinburgh till the end of January as planned. I truly hope that one day, in years to come, that brave young girl is sitting under the starry sky on a warm Australian evening, telling her grandchildren about her adventures in Europe . Vainly, I hope that she tells them about the time when she met a strange man, who told her the story that motivated her to stay. Her heart longing to visit those places again, just once before she dies.

After speaking to the girl, I decided to go for a wander around Edinburgh. See if I could get myself a job or fall into my destiny somehow. As I left the hostel and turned to walk up the steep little side street that led to the Royal Mile I saw a strange sight. At the top of the street looking down toward me stood a man that looked like he had no place in this picture. He was wearing orange robes that blew mysteriously in the wind. I walked to the top of the street and as I passed him, I noticed how tall he was. He must have been about 6ft 6. He had baggy orange robes and sandals on his large feet. I stopped, looked up at him and asked "Are you dressed like that for a reason, or is it a fashion statement?" He explained that he was a Buddhist Monk and these are the robes of his religion. He told me that he had been a monk for over thirty years, and that he came here from America. We walked up the Royal Mile together for a way and I remember that we spoke for some time, but honestly, I only remember one thing that he said. He told me that he didn't use any animal products, that he respected animals as he respected all life. I pondered this for a second or two as I continued walking, but when I turned to respond to him... he had gone.

I wanted to ask him what I could have to do to become a monk myself. I thought god maybe wanted me to be one. I paced the city streets, checking taxi ranks, asking strangers if they had seen the man in the orange robes, but he was nowhere to be seen. I began to think that he had never been there at all. Maybe I had imagined him.

Maybe he was god himself.

I wasn't sure what to think, but somehow afterwards something within me changed. I felt a deep need to go home, a panic that I wasn't there with my family. I needed to leave, but in this moment I was so overwhelmed and I needed help. I noticed a nearby cathedral, ran inside, and I sat and prayed for guidance. I wept bitterly in this moment, thinking about my family, thinking about Dobby, but most of all I was thinking about the terrible things that I had done to animals that had been in my care.

I made it through the rest of the day with a heavy heart. I didn't sleep well, and I lay awake as guilt and sadness plagued my heart. I was silently weeping for hours, saddened about leaving my family, about losing my old friend Dobby, about the cruelty I had caused and was still causing to the animals in my care.

I decided that it was time to contact my wife.

I remembered that I had seen a bank of payphones down the road, so I walked through the icy air and called home. As I waited for an answer I remembered that a nearby shop was playing bagpipe music and that the phone box had a strange smell of urine. My wife answered the phone, and to my surprise she was genuinely pleased to hear from me. She told me to come home, that everything was OK. She asked me when she should expect me home and I answered that I would be home around evening time. She seemed very surprised at this,

"Where are you?"

She gasped. I told her I was in Edinburgh and that I was sorry for the worry that I must have caused her. We chatted a while longer and then I went back to the hostel, collected my things and checked out. I had slept just 5 nights there, but I had changed more in that time than I did in my whole life before it.

I made my way to Waverley Station. I just felt so relieved to be going home. Somehow I was new and revived, and as I neared the station a homeless man asked me if I had any loose change.

I smiled, reached into my pocket and passed him a handful of screwed up notes. I don't know how much I gave him, but he was happy with it, because I heard him shout after me, thanking me most excitedly.

I bought a ticket to Carlisle and waited on a bench for the train to arrive as a little treat, I decided that I would in fact purchase first class this time around. I needed food too, as I had been on very small rations for almost two weeks. Most of all, I was full of excitement to see my family, and my sadness for Dobby had turned to sadness for all the animals that I had encountered in my harsh life.

When I got to Carlisle, I bought a ticket to Skipton. I found that I had a full hour to wait, so I went to buy my wife a gift. I looked into the windows of many jewellery shops, hoping to find something that might fit the moment. It was when I looked into the window of Thomas Sabo, that I noticed a silver angel wing necklace. I was now low on money because the train tickets were quite expensive and I had given a large amount of money to the homeless man, but I went inside anyway. I enquired how much the necklace was and the assistant took it from the display and scanned a little tag that was on it. "£19.00," she told me. I was very surprised, and I asked if the chain was included, and it was. I had no idea why it was so cheap, when everything else in the shop seemed so expensive, but nonetheless I paid for the necklace and popped it into my grubby coat pocket before making my way back to the station.

I finally made it home at about 8 pm, it was dark, and cold. My children were all waiting for me and all came and hugged me on my arrival. My wife cried and flung her arms around me. I received a hero's welcome and it was far, far more than I deserved. I can say that my wife has never shown me any anger about my 'running away from home' as I like to call it. Instead she jokes about it. Every year since then we have had an annual visit to Edinburgh and we probably always will. Whatever happens to me there changed my whole life and I have never eaten meat again from the day I returned. I sold my flock of sheep and turned my back on farming. I never trained another horse nor owned one.

I did give my wife her necklace and though I wouldn't tell her how much I paid; she loved it and she still wears it, every single day. She later told me she had researched how much it cost. It was on the Thomas Sabo website at a little under £200.00. How it came to me for £19.00 ,how I came to meet a buddhist monk, how this journey managed to change my life, I will never really know. I could always, of course, chalk it down to God's will.

CHAPTER FOUR: COWS

Not so fun fact: There are 1.85 million dairy cows in the UK. There are 7.75 million beef cattle and young stock in the UK. Cows are usually slaughtered using a captive-bolt that stuns them. They are then shackled by their hind legs, raised and then their throats are cut to bleed out.

I have, personally, seen injured cattle slaughtered on site as they had outgrown their usage. The cow was stunned with a captive bolt pistol, and her throat was slit. Some sort of rod was shoved down her neck and spine, and repeatedly in and out. This made the her body jiggle about hauntingly. I think this was done to help bleed the animal, but honestly, I am not sure. What I do know is that both beef and dairy cows end their life this way.

Sweet cows and bulls and baby calves,

You have seen me

You have heard me

I beg forgiveness for all that I have done.

When we meet again, may my eyes see straight,
and may I feel no shame.

The warmth of the summer sun was draped over my body like a welcome blanket as I lay at the side of the pasture. The sound of the dairy cows munching the fresh green grass only a few metres from me was meditative. In the distance the cuckoo's lugubrious tones gave a melancholy feel to that June afternoon. I drifted into dormancy and all my earthly worries melted into the vast expanse of the unconscious. If I had never awakened from this slumber and my soul had left my body, and if my earthly years were spent; then what a perfect end that would have been. Instead I was ripped from this utopia by a sharp kick in the thigh and a loud shout,

"Get up, you lazy little shit. I've been looking for you. We've got calves to de-horn."

My father scolded me until I was up on my feet. My peace was over for that day, and the manor of which I was woken put me into a foul mood. If you have dairy cows, or beef cows, bulls, or bullocks (castrated bulls); you don't want them to grow up with horns. That would be dangerous to the farmers, as you can imagine. So, when they are calves you would burn off the horn buds with a red hot copper de-budding iron. This often involved me holding the calf in a headlock, while my dad burned the horn buds off.

No problem, right?

A bit of anaesthetic; and Bob's your uncle!

Well...Think again.

There was no vet involved, so no anaesthetic was used. Whether this was legal or not, I couldn't have told you at the time, but believe me, this did happen. It happened behind closed barn doors more than you can imagine, it may still happen to this day, somewhere.

Have I mentioned that farming is a business, an industry, so it's all about pounds and pence? The vets were too expensive to pay to come and de-bud 10 or 15 calves. Think of it like this: if a calf is worth £150, and the vet charges £50 per calf to remove the horns, then over 10 calves equates to £500. We could have them done in an hour ourselves, and save £500. A no-brainer, really. That's how farming works: pounds and pence. I have never met a farmer that put animals over profit. Actually, now that I come to think of it there was one. He was the local joke among the farmers. "Treats his livestock like pets" they would sneer. Please notice the word livestock, it backs up the pounds and pence truth that I have mentioned.

So we burnt the buds off and the calves bellowed out in pain and fear as I held tight the smell of the burning hair and flesh would choke in the back of my throat and make my eyes water, but cruelly I didn't cast a thought to the pain of the poor little baby cows. It always took three or four attempts per bud to get them completely off. There was no quiet calm farmer smiling down at those animals saying " that'll do calf... that'll do!".

You may have all heard stories of calves being taken off cows as soon as they are born. You might have even heard that this happens only in the dairy industry. Well it's all a load of rubbish. It happens in both industries, and let me tell you why. Most dairy cows are impregnated with beef breed bulls. You only impregnated your very best cows with dairy bulls because the beef cross breeds could be worth over £200.00 more than a dairy calf, if it turned out to be a bull calf. Complicated, I know. I will explain a little clearer.

You impregnated your best cows with an expensive dairy bull sperm, hoping the cow would produce a female calf so you could rear it to around 2-3 years old, impregnate it; and when it has had a calf bring it into the dairy herd. However, if the cow you pregnated with the expensive dairy bull sperm has a male calf, then it had to be sold on and was worth less than half of the price that a beef breed would be worth. All make sense now? It's the pounds and pence thing again.

That is why most dairy cows were impregnated with beef breed sperm, and as soon as that cow had its baby, we took it away from the cow. We did let the calf have one feed from its mother to get the colostrum, but then we took it away. The mother would frantically try and stay with her baby, and would stand at the gate crying for her, for up to 4 or 5 days. Eventually, she gave up and joined the herd. Can you imagine the panic the poor mother was going through? What emotions she must have been experiencing?

If another cow in the herd had a calf in the field, the newer mothers would gather round, probably to see if it was their calf, and the bellows would start again. It was a bit of a nuisance the cows coming to the gate crying for their babies. Kept us awake!

Let's look at how you impregnate a cow with sperm. Well, the artificial inseminator would come to your farm. He would then put on his overalls and a long disposable glove. He would then get a straw of whatever sperm you ordered from a flask of liquid nitrogen in the back of his vehicle. Next he would load the straw into a long syringe.

Later he would shove his hand up the cow's anus to about the center of his bicep. He would then feel around for something. I didn't know what it was, but when he found it he would shove the straw up the vagina and squirt the sperm up.

The cow would arch its back with pain and more often than not, bellow out. When the calves were taken from their mother they were put into little pens and we would teach them to drink milk from a bucket. To do this we would let the calves suck our fingers, lower their little heads into the warm powdered milk replacer, and then slowly remove your fingers. The calves would take a few days to learn to drink the milk from a bucket without having to use your fingers, but I would find that a few good punches on the nose stopped them trying to find your fingers.

Now in the mid 80's to mid 90's the veil export trade really took off. You could get good money for a Belgium Blue cross dairy cow bill calf. It was like a gold rush. Everyone was impregnating their dairy cows with the Belgium Blue bull. You could make money hand over fist and by now you know that farming is all about the money.

There was one problem, the calves were much bigger than regular calves. They were actually born with muscles. This, of course, means difficult births. Never mind because the calves are worth more, you can afford the vet. Yes, in theory this is true, but did I mention farming is a business, so it's pounds and pence. Let's save money and deliver the calves ourselves.

Now when a cow was in labor you would stick your hand inside and have a feel around, make sure the calf was the right way round and didn't have a leg back. If all was ok, you could probably leave the cow to have the calf on its own. Remember though, we are now impregnating cows with beef bulls like the Belgium blue, and even if these calves were all in the correct position they would still get stuck. If this happened you would tie two ropes to the unborn calf's front feet and you would pull and pull. The cow would drop to the floor and cry out in pain but you had to pull. If it stuck for too long it could die, and that could be £500 that is lost with the life of the calf. On more than one occasion, my father fastened the ropes to the tractor and pulled the calf out. He figured if he didn't he would lose it anyway. I can hear the bellows of the cows even now. I remember on one occasion that we lost both the cow and calf in a way, that I won't tell you in case it haunts you like it haunts me. How could he think that was a good idea? I don't know, but it was all in a day's work back then. There was a lot of death on the farm with animals during birthing, and with it a lot of bad temper.

I have often kicked cows and calves in temper; punched and kicked animals when they weren't doing what I wanted them to do, we all did. It was part of farming. A lot of farmers carried sticks around with them to administer a punishment if things were not going their way. It was around this time I first experienced my first vegan. It was a guy called Spider from the soap opera 'Coronation Street'. He was a gangly pale stereotypical vegan, and I hated him. I wanted to punch him every time I saw him. If I could have looked into the future and seen myself as a vegan, I would have probably hung myself there and then. My father hated him, so I did.

One time my father had forgotten to de-bud a batch of cattle, so of course their horns grew far too big to burn off. Job for the vet! Yes, you're probably thinking 'at last! The vet!' No, did I not mention farming is about pounds and pence, like any other business so the vet wasn't called that day. Instead my father got out the hacksaw and tied the bullocks by the neck and started to saw off the horns. We kids were there to try and help but at this time I was around 7 years old and the twins around 13 my oldest sister was probably at work as she was 17. My dads temper flared as the first bullock squirted blood all over his face, from the half sawn through horn. The bullock cried out and struggled in its pain. My father left and returned in a temper frenzy with a large hammer and knocked off the half decapitated horn. He was bashing the other one off without sawing it when one of his friends appeared and calmed him down. The other bullocks were crying out in fear and running around wildly. We children had hidden out of the way, trying our best not to get trampled. And the poor young bullock had to be cut free. I was taken into the house and I could still hear the cries from the animals as I went. I didn't know to this day what ever happened to the poor fellow.

Now, farmers have received subsidies over the years. Our farm was a small farm, so didn't receive much in subsidies, but bigger farms received more. Good news for the animals: more money to pay the vet's bill... Wrong again. Most farmers show off their wealth with a fancy new tractor, or a new steel framed building; a Land Rover; or a shiny new Ifor Williams Trailer. The animals got much the same treatment, whatever the income.

Out of the blue, father decided to give me and the twins a calf of our own. The idea was that we reared it and when it was old enough it would be sold for beef, and we would put the money in the bank and start a bank account. No one can argue that my father really did want the best for us, and I was eager to please him.

I called my calf Patch. He was a Heriford cross Fresian bullock. Over the next 18 months, I watched him grow and formed somewhat of a bond with him. The time came for us to sell him, and I prepared myself. I was quite excited about having a bank account though. The evening before he was due to leave for the cattle market, I overheard my father telling my mother that he would have to keep the money to help pay for the twins' 21st birthday party, that they had requested.

The next morning I helped load Patch into the trailer. I looked at my father, and I told him to keep the money to help pay for my sister's party. He thanked me and agreed that it would be a good help. At this time he was starting to recover from his depression. I was truly programmed into the farming mind set by now. I was more sad about the loss of money, than the loss of Patch. I had become a shy 15 year old farmer.

The Milk Industry

Milk is inspected for quality, this includes the amount of butterfat, the bacterial count, antibiotics in the milk, and water content. This may come as a surprise, and not a pleasant one, but all the above are present in the milk that you drink, that is, if you drink cows milk. Let me explain in a little more detail.

1. Butterfat defines the creaminess of the milk. In the milk industry, it is good to have more butter fat. The more butter fat in milk, the more you get paid (pence per litre).

2. Bacterial count defines the amount of mastitis present in the milk. Mastitis is an inflammation in the udder tissue in a cow, and is most often due to an infection. With this, one or more of the cows udders become swollen and sore. They then fill with puss and hard lumps of infected matter. This is treated by antibiotics. The bacteria count indicates how much of this puss is present in the milk. Unfortunately, there is an 'acceptable' amount of puss that is allowed in the milk you drink.

3. Antibiotics in the milk, is exactly as it sounds. This is how much antibiotic is present in the milk. If there is too much antibiotic present, it affects the cheese making process. In very simple terms, antibiotics will kill the bacteria that makes the cheese. Again, there is an 'acceptable' percentage of antibiotic allowed in milk.

4. Water is always present in milk. With water making up 87% of its content. So, if your milk contains more than this, which it often does, it has likely been watered down.

My father had perfected a way to send high butterfat milk in large amounts, with low antibiotics and low bacterial and water content. However, this was not achieved by following the rules. Following the rules costs money, and farming is about pounds and pence. Instead, his amazing record was set by bending the rules. This is how it was done.

My fathers dairy herd was mostly Holstein cattle. The Holstein Friesian is a breed of dairy cattle that originated in the Dutch provinces of North Holland and Friesland, as well as in Schleswig-Holstein in Northern Germany. These cows produced a large amount of milk, but their butterfat content is low, so their milk quality is low. My father got around this by incorporating four or five Jersey cows into the herd. Jersey cows don't produce as much milk, but the milk that they do produce is extremely high in butterfats. The presence of Jersey cow milk in the tank considerably increases the overall milk quality . By doing this, my father was able to increase his profit. Although this may not be considered ethical, it perfectly legal.

Regarding the bacteria-count, my father also utilised some rule-bending practices. You may remember that I told you that the more bacteria present in the milk, the less you get paid. The idea for this test is that if you had a cow that was suffering from mastitis, you would keep her milk out of the tank until she was better. However, this means throwing milk away, and subsequently, losing money. The way round this was to know what day the milk purchasing company was going to test your milk. Once a week, the purchasing company would take a sample of milk before it was sucked from the tank and into the milk collection wagon. Unfortunately for us, they did this on random days, so you had no idea when this would be done.

The company that we used tested all the local farms on the same day. It just so happened that from the field at the far west of our farm we had a perfect view of our neighbours dairy. It also just so happened that they collected their milk before they collected ours. This meant that it was my job at 8.30 every morning, to take an expensive pair of binoculars to the top of the field, and watch our neighbours milk being collected. By doing this, I could clearly see if the tanker driver was testing the milk. If he was testing, then we would leave the infected milk out. If he wasn't testing, we would pour the infected milk into the tank. I was very good at keeping myself unseen. Therefore, the milk that we distributed was riddled with bacteria.

You have probably already guessed, that this is how we managed to get around the antibiotic and water content tests too. You may be wondering why there would ever be a high water content in the milk. Well as you might expect, it's all to make money.

I have already mentioned that farmers are paid pence per litre, and in the old days the tank that your milk was stored in had a dipstick in it. The milk wagon driver would simply check the dipstick to see how much milk was in your tank and log it down. This of course, needed to be accurate. So, when your milk storage tank is installed, an official from the milk collection company will check that the tank was set up and calibrated correctly.

My father, however, had a hydraulic jack hidden in the dairy. Before the milk collection wagon arrived, he would use the jack to lift the tank a little at one side. This would make the milk flow towards the dipstick and give the impression that there was more milk in the tank than there actually was. We were not the only farmers to do this, and soon the milk collection company changed to a flow meter.

The flow meter measured the amount of milk that was in your tank as it entered the collection wagon. Now, the only way around this was to add water to the milk. This could easily be done when it was not a test day, and you know that me and my binoculars could predict that quite easily. My father would add 20 litres of water per 100 litres of milk, so 20% of the milk was water.

One local farm got caught doing this and was prosecuted. This farmer had two sons. He sent a large amount of milk, and it would take quite some time to transfer the milk from his large tank to the collection wagon. The farmer would invite the driver into the house for tea and biscuits, while the milk transferred automatically and the flow meter measured the amount of milk transferred. This became the drivers regular tea break and when he was absent, the relief drivers would do the same thing.

While the drivers were having tea, the farmer's two sons would tip containers of water into the tank and water down the milk. This went on for years, until one cold November morning when the driver had a trainee with him. The young driver was a little shy, and told the driver he would stay in the wagon while he went into the house for tea. The driver didn't mention this to the farmer, so they had no idea he was there. After some time, the trainee got out of the wagon and decided to watch the tank empty. It was then that he saw the two burly farmer's sons pouring gallons of water into the tank. That is how this particular farmer got caught.

To summarize, concerning the milk that you might pour on your cornflakes in a morning: around 87% (sometimes more) is water, the rest is made up of butter fat, mastitis puss, and antibiotics. All of which are legally allowed in your milk.

CHAPTER FIVE: SHEEP

Not so fun fact: There are 33 million sheep in the UK. Almost all sheep end their lives for human consumption. Sheep are killed by, head-to-back stun-kill, (electric stun), or captive bolt stun. They are then shackled, their throats cut to bleed them out.

A friend should see all things, not just what he wants to see.

I didn't want to see your pain, nor tears or hear your cry.

Forgive my deliberate blindness.

Forgive the lies that I told myself.

And when the setting sun takes me with her, may I come to you better than when we last met.

It had been a severe winter that year. The snow came in late November and stayed till the end of February.

The sheep had suffered terribly due to the lack of nutrition. The grass was covered and we were low on forage for the dairy cows, so we couldn't spare much for the heavily pregnant sheep. Maybe we had over-stocked the land, but we had already lost half a dozen sheep and there was no sign of a let-up in the cold spell. My father bought mineral blocks and concentrate sheep pellets to supplement their diet.

He had invested a lot of money in buying the sheep at the end of October and it pained him to see them dying. I don't know how many sheep we lost that winter but I remember we dug a lot of graves. It cost money to have the dead sheep collected so we just buried them in the field. It wasn't exactly legal but money is money and every little saving adds up.

I remember the death of one sheep In particular. I have tried to forget it, or at least tuck it away in the back of my mind; but every now and then I recall it.

The cold East wind blew the stinging snow across the flat field into our faces, as we crouched over a heavily pregnant sheep that was in labor. My father had been rummaging around inside her, with his thick cold arm. Her bleats of pain were carried away by the unforgiving wind.

The sheep had prolapsed for the third time within a month. My father diagnosed this by the rotten smell coming from her, that the lambs had died some days before. The sheep had prolapsed several days before, and my father had tried to make a temporary fix to hold her inners from coming out. To do this he had got a strong needle that he made from a 6 inch nail and some strong thread.

He had shoved the lining back into her vagina and put two stitches in to hold the lining in place. This is probably when the unborn lambs died inside of her. Now she was in so much pain that my father had given up on her. He sent me up to the farm to get the crowbar. The crow bar was a 5 foot long two inch thick iron bar with a pointed end. We usually used it for loosening stones when digging holes and such.

When I got back to the sheep and my father, he took the bar and thrust it hard into the forehead of the sheep in an attempt to kill her. Anyone who knows about sheep know that they have a very strong forehead: and it took him several blows to kill her. I found this very disturbing, at the time and I was very upset.

There is a saying in the farming community that the main ambition of a sheep is to die. They say this because there are so many deaths while the sheep are pregnant and in labor. Now, many times the lambs would die while being born. Leaving a sheep with lots of milk and no lambs to drink it, and sometimes a sheep would have three or even 4 lambs, and she would not have enough milk to feed them. This seems like an obvious solution. Take a lamb off the one with three and give it to the one with none.

This would be great, but unfortunately sheep recognise their lambs by smell so they won't accept another sheep's lamb so easily.

Farmers have a solution though. They would take the skins off the mothers dead babies and put them onto the spare lamb of another sheep, so when the lamb drank, the mother would turn and smell the skin of her own babies. This works and after a few days of drinking her milk they take on the mother's smell and the lamb or lambs are accepted. Imagine if we did this with humans, or even cats or dogs. There would be an uproar.

The male lambs need to be castrated and all the lambs need their tails docking. The main reason for this is because they are worth more if this is done. It's that pounds and pence thing again. Sheep with docked tails keep cleaner and are at a reduced risk of getting maggots that start to eat the lambs alive if not treated. The males need castrating so they get fatter quicker and don't impregnate the females when they get a little older.

This is done by putting tight rubber rings around the testicles and the tails. The little newborn lambs will lie on the floor and bleed in pain for a few hours in some cases. Eventually the pain wears off and over the next month the tails and testicles just drop off. If the rings are put on within the first few hours of life the pain seems to be much less than it is for a lamb that is left for a week or so before they are done.

I have seen both the removal of testicles and the tails done with a sharp knife and a lot of blood. When the lambs get fat enough which is anywhere between 5 and 12 months, they are taken either to the auction mart or directly to the slaughter house.

I have worked in an auction mart and have seen the lambs crammed into pens. It used to be that a grader would examine them and if they were properly fat to the right standards they would receive the grade. The grader would get his assistant to punch penny size holes in their ears. They would just bleed all over each other. Then they would be sent into the ring and sent round where the butchers would bid for them. There would be butchers buying for supermarkets like Morrisons and butchers, buying to sell to small high street shops. The lambs would eventually be crammed onto wagons and sent to slaughter. Their mothers left behind at the farm bleeding and searching for their precious babies. It makes me angry now when I see meat eaters looking into the fields and admiring the little lambs at play. That privilege should be reserved for a time when eating meat is banned.

They say that animals can't speak, but for those of us who know them, understand that they speak a universal language.

They feel the same emotions as us; jealousy, anger, sadness, happiness, pain, fear and most of all: love.

These emotions are all you need to communicate.

CHAPTER SIX: PIGS

Not so fun fact: There are 5.2 million pigs in the UK. Pigs are killed by gas-stunning. This involves using gas mixtures, usually high concentrations of carbon dioxide. The pigs can be heard screaming as the gas is administered. This is one of the most upsetting deaths to hear or see. They are shackled and gutted very quickly.

You trusted me to keep you safe.

Our smiling eyes met many times, I fed you and laughed with love.

I led you to pain,

I led you to fear,

A strong heart does not beat lies,

Shame is my companion

Forgive my weak heart and feeble tongue.

When the shadows clear and light fills the darkness.

You will find me a better man.

Till then I will make kindness my business.

I will be your voice and speak your words.

One cold but sunny April afternoon, just after dinner. I went for a ramble on the moors a few miles west of the farm. There was an old tumble-down barn just behind a bank of spruce trees. I often explored it and imagined what it was like when it was in good repair. It was an unusual barn because in the middle of the far wall was a fireplace. It was quite ornate in its design and it looked out of place in such a basic building. I imagine there was a simple explanation for it being there, but I couldn't think of one that satisfied my curiosity. I would usually search for clues or signs that would shed light on this little mystery and then turn for home. However, on this occasion I decided to walk a little further across the heather, following sheep paths that made the trekking easier. I had wandered further than I had ever been on that moor. I felt excited, but a little worried also. After a while I came across a steep culvert and I peered down its steep banks. In the bottom I could see a small cluster of buildings and a area of land that was fenced into a small Croft. The Croft was black and boggy and I could see what seemed to be pigs moving around. I wanted to get a closer look. I had never seen pigs outside before. I had only ever seen them in a sty on my neighbour's farm.

I cautiously made my way down the banks to the fence of the muddy little croft. I was correct, there were two mother pigs each with a litter of piglets. I watched the piglets skip and play. They formed little gangs and ran around in the cool sunlight. It reminded me of my friends at school playing at break time. The mother pigs rummaged through the mud with their powerful snouts. I watched them for a while until one of the mothers spotted me and called the piglets back to her. This alerted the other mother pig and she did the same. I had never seen pigs relatively free before. I had never seen piglets play nor mothers be protective.

They seemed almost human in their behaviour and it gave me a warm happy feeling. I took one last look at these happy little families and turned for home before the owner of the small-holding spotted me.

I only have one story about my own pigs and this one hurts me as equally as the others. I was 12 years old and I was with my friend who bred pigs. One of his sows was giving birth and I watched with interest. The sow was in a small crate and I watched as she gave birth to 10 or 12 little piglets.

Two of them were very small runts and my friend said they will die and that it would be better to kill them now so the stronger ones had more chance to do well. I asked my friend to spare them and that I would buy the piglets off him. I think that I offered him £12 each, and rather than lose out he agreed to the sale. I ran back home and persuaded my father to let me have them. I brought them home to a small makeshift pen and nursed them back to good health. I knew their fate but carried on all the same. One day my father decided that these two young males needed castrating. We needed to do them that day before they got too big to handle. You will have suspected by now that these little piggies were not going to meet the vet. Instead my dad sent me to the bathroom to bring down a razor blade. Not one of the razors that you would find in a Turkish barber's shop. No, just one of the little blades that was wrapped in paper from one of those sliding plastic packs. I gave him the razor and he told me to hold the pigs by the back legs. I held on tight to the back legs and my father slit the scrotum and popped out the testicles. He then cut them off. The pigs squeezed and struggled but I held tight. When they were both done my father got the removed testicles and threw them into the pig pen. The pigs ate them all up. I didn't really know what to make of this. It gave me a strange uneasy feeling deep in the pit of my stomach. I remember lying awake some nights, confused with the strange menacing sensation in my body as I thought about the pigs unknowingly eating parts of their own body. It didn't seem right then. I can only feel antipathy now. The poor pigs never saw the outside world until the day they were loaded into the trailer and sent to slaughter.

As I sit and write these awful memories, I look back at that time. How I wish that I could have been aware of their mistreatment. If I could only have let them into the fields to rummage and frolic, just like the pigs I had seen years before. I have taken for granted my freedom, the privilege of feeling the sun on my skin and the fresh sweet smells of the summer foliage. To wander freely, without fences nor boundaries, without shackles or chains to keep me in subjugation. Should not all beings experience these things as stock?

CHAPTER SEVEN: HENS

Not so fun fact: There are 124 million broiler chickens,(Chickens reared for their meat), in the uk and their are 16 million chickens still caged for egg production. Chickens are usually killed by electric water bath. The chickens are shackled by their feet, on a kind of conveyor system. They then pass through the electric water bath which stuns them. They then have their throats cut. Even the egg producing chickens end up in the human consumption food chain as soups, stocks or stews.

I dare say that stranger tales have been told than this one, but in the pond that it swims, it is truly a fantastic creature.

On hot summer days at the old farm, the air was fragrant with the smell of the lavender that grew under the apple trees in the orchard. The blackbirds would sweetly whistle their melodies from the large, old cherry tree that stood crookedly at the side of the farmhouse, and the chickens would shower themselves in warm dry soil; their chicks would peck and scratch around their mothers.

The cockerels would stand alert and vainly crow out their authority over the brood. The world was a happy place for them. But this pretty little picture was not meant to last. Thought these chickens had relative freedom compared to their caged relatives, there was hard times ahead of these souls too.

How many hens I have killed, plucked, gutted and eaten I can't remember. I can still feel their necks crack in my hands and the aftershock of flaps subside with their life force. My father used to breed and show Old English Game hens. He didn't keep them for their eggs, though we did get a lot of eggs from them. He didn't breed them for their flesh, though we would eat one or two of them every Sunday. He did however, breed them to pop into traveling boxes and take them around the country to different shows. Personally, I can't think of a more pointless hobby, with the exception of golf, or watching football, or horse racing... ok maybe it's equally pointless as all hobbies; in keeping with the opinion of the audience.

Most of the hens were free range, and I mean free range. Not like the egg producers free range, those hens live in massive crowded barns and very rarely venture outside. There just has to be a door open to the outside for the business to be awarded a free range certificate.Trust me, only a tiny percentage of the thousand or more hens in the shed venture outside. Why? Because their feed is inside the building.

No, my father's hens wandered through the fields around the farm, they loved to scratch in the dry soil. They pecked at insects and foliage and had a jolly good time.

Old English Game chickens are similar the Pheasants. They are not as tame as the more domesticated breeds. The males were used for fighting in times of old. People used to win and lose large amounts of money gambling on these birds. It was banned in the UK in 1835, but underground circles still fight them today.

My father only wanted the chickens for show purposes though. His chickens, was his great passion in life.

He made all sorts of acquaintances at the shows from all over the country. Now, with all popular hobbies there is a terminology and language that the participants use. For example you would not say a chicken had nice eyes, you would say that the chicken has a good eye, singular. You would not say the chicken has a nice formation. You would say it is good in the hand. He would often get visits from other people who participated in the same hobby, and they would spend hours talking about hens and cocks, pullets and cock-chickens; standards and bantams. He would get phone calls from people all over the country. They could talk about their game birds for hours on the telephone. I would hear my father telling the person on the other end, that he had a very nice cock at the moment and that it had a good eye. He would say it felt good in the hand and the next time that they visited he would get it out and they could have a feel. This was normal talk on a Sunday afternoon telephone conversation in our home. It was traditional to remove the comb and other tissue around the face of the male birds. This is called dubbing.

To do this using a sharp pair of scissors, you would clip the comb as close to the head as possible, following the curvature of the head. There was No anesthetic and the cockerel would need to be held tightly while it struggled in pain. My father would put cobwebs over the wounds to stop the bleeding. The dubbing was originally done to fighting cockerels to reduce the amount of blood that would temporarily blind the fighting birds and render them unable to fight. They are dubbed today in keeping with tradition. It has no other purpose.

The trouble with game chickens being free range is that the hens would sneak away to hidden nooks and crannies to make their nests. If you couldn't find their nests, the hen would one day appear with a clutch of newly hatched baby chicks. This was ok, but they were pretty hard to look after. If conditions were wet and cold you would often find dead or dying baby chicks around the farm yard. If you found an almost dead chick it could often be revived by warmth. We often had baby chicks in cut-down cereal boxes in front of the open coal fire.

I remember one particular wet November evening, we were all sat in the living room in front of the fire and probably watching CoronationStreet. I heard a squeaking sound. I looked around the room to seek the culprit of the sound. There was nothing. Then my sister heard it. It seemed to be near my father's chair. He heard it too and promptly stood up and looked around. We could see nothing, but the sound became more frequent and louder. All off a sudden something startled my father, and he put his hand in his trouser pocket. He rummaged around and pulled out two baby chicks. They squeaked and wobbled around in his hand. He looked down at them and calmly and said," I thought these were dead". He put on his flat cap and went outside to put them back with their mother.

You may find it strange that the warmth had revived them, but is it not stranger still, that he was sitting watching television with a pocket full of dead chicks in the first place? Bonnie and Clyde were the names of two broiler chickens that I once accidentally rescued. Now when I say accidentally, I mean I opened a box that had been left in the farmyard and in it was two large white chickens. One of them was a cockerel and the other was a hen. I had no idea how or why they were in a large box in the farmyard, but later I found out that they were a gift from my brother-in-law. He had been working in a large broiler farm, helping to clean the main building out. The owner had gifted him four large white broiler chickens for his good work. He had kept two for himself ; which he quickly killed and plucked and had dropped two off for my father.

Their fat would have been identical to their unfortunate companions if I had not stumbled across them. My father had been given the two chickens and left them in the yard. He had intended to kill and dress them ready for Sunday lunch. However, he had been side tracked by a more pressing engagement of which I have no idea. But luckily for the two mistreated companions, I had stumbled across them. On finding the box and discovering it's contents, I tipped them out onto the floor and had expected them to run away. This did not happen. The two chickens just sat on the floor. I was amazed by how big they were. They were the size of three of the Old English Game birds. I gave one a little push with my wellington boot, but I discovered that they couldn't walk at all. Just about then my father showed up. He explained how he had forgotten about them and it was a good job I found them or they would have been in the box all night. Like me he was surprised at the size of the chickens.

However, he was not surprised that they couldn't walk. He explained that they are so cramped together from being chicks that they have never had the room to walk.

All of a sudden Clyde shuffle l forward and started pecking at a dock leaf that was sprouting from a crack in the concrete yard. Mr father said that would be the first time that the chicken had seen a green leaf. Clyde made a strange clucking noise and it summoned Bonnie to come and have a peck. She tried to shuffle forward but struggled more than Clyde. She did finally get there and my father wondered if in time they could walk. This curiosity had given Bonnie and Clyde a reprieve . Their death sentence was postponed. We put Bonnie and close in a large pen with a tin-sheet shelter at one side. It had a high fence around it. Not to stop hen's getting out, but to stop foxes getting in. They were safe in there and they happily shuffled around pecking at grass and the wheat that I would feed them, I decided to be their guardian.

I fed them wheat and made sure their water was full. After about a month the chickens could manage a wobble, which was a cross between a shuffle and a walk. Clyde had started to get amorous with Bonnie and it was about this time that I gave them their names. By two months at the farm they could fully walk and they were happy rescued chickens. I was really happy that they had recovered and they became my pets. I fed them and put clean straw in their shelter. I would let them eat bread dipped in milk from my fingers and as soon as they saw me they ran to the cage door; yes, I said ran. They could run now. I really did love those chickens One October my mother went to stay at my nana's house for a week and she took me with her. I loved my nana and didn't protest about it. My father said that he would look after Bonnie and Clyde while I was gone. I had a great time at my nana's house and time passed quickly.

On my return I eventually wandered to the pen to see Bonnie and Clyde. Of course they had gone. I went to the house to ask my father where they had gone, but the smiles on my sister's face said it all. My father had killed them on the day that I left. He had plucked and dressed them and he and my three sisters had eaten them while I had been away. I admit, I truly wanted to cry, but I would never give them the satisfaction of seeing me do that.

Throughout my lifetime, I have visited barn chicken farms, I have visited battery chicken farms; I have also visited, "so-called", free range egg farms and I can honestly say that the chickens on our farm, though they had their tribulations, had a much nicer life than any of them.

CHAPTER EIGHT: WILDLIFE

Not so fun fact: Managing fox and crow numbers is part of sheep farming. It has become a tradition . Many farmer's livelihoods rely on selling the lambs for meat or to continue their breeding . For farmers lambing outside in the fields, they claim that crows and foxes cause havoc among flocks, so they must be killed and controlled. This also applies to magpies, mink and other wildlife depending on the livestock that is being farmed.

It's rather like using pesticides to kill certain insects that damage crops. I personally don't think that any of the above is necessary and that this is avoidable. However, many creatures are accidentally killed when harvesting crops for animal feed and human consumption. I don't think that this is avoidable, but that's just my personal view.

> *Let the wolves lie still for a while and enjoy the soft, warm sun, Let the children play for a while, for everyone needs fun.*

> *So let the wolves lie still for a while, the sun will make them sleep.*

> *And let the children play for a while, for what we sow we reap.*

To live in the countryside from infancy to adulthood is to become at one with it. My teachers were the fox and the owl, the deer and badger, the stoat and the mink. Silent teachers, who's intelligence and cunning I came to understand and respect. Each season dictates your habits. You know the wilderness around you and anticipate the changes. You feel the storm before the first dark cloud, you feel the spring on a snowy February morning and sense the winter on a warm August afternoon. You become as the creatures that share this terrain with you.

When I was a hunter as a boy I was more stealth than even the fox. I could move unseen by most eyes. No creature would hear me nor smell me if I so wished. I could even get the creatures to hunt for me, yet so could all who was brought up like me, and some much better than I.

To give you an example of knowing the wildlife. I had been watching a company of stoats that had made home near the farm. I had watched their courtship. I had watched them mate and I watched them disappear. Stoats are solitary creatures, they come together only to mate, so I knew that soon they would have a litter kits. This means the mother would be hunting rabbits. To watch a mother stoat hunt is a mesmerising and haunting thing to see. The stoat will spot the rabbit and instead of creeping or stalking her prey, the stoat will skip around the rabbit in large circles. The rabbit watches, maybe intrigued or enchanted by the movement. The circles, however, are ever decreasing and in time the rabbit knows it is in danger and will freeze. The scared rabbit will let out a piercing scream as the stoat moves in and then grabs the petrified creature. She quickly kills it and drags it back to her kits. (That dance is sometimes called the dance of death).

Now if you know she is working a particular area quite close to her den, which by the way, is often the home of her former prey. You can watch and wait. The scream of the rabbit will call you in, and if you are sharp, you get the rabbit before the stoat moves in.

A quick bang on the back of the head and it's rabbit for tea. No snares set, no bullets used. The stoat will soon catch another one for her young. That's how to use nature to help you survive in the wild.

I knew every foxes den in the area. I knew their paths and when they would walk them. I loved to see the foxes and I kept their whereabouts strictly to myself. If my father knew where they were he would get someone in to kill them. He would protect his prizewinning hens at all costs.

Even now I can walk in the countryside and smell the fox has been near. A little more investigation and I have found her path. Within the hour I would find her den. I fancied myself as being like the fox as a child. I would roam the hedgerows in silence, unseen with my air rifle as I hunted pheasant. I was a killer and a menace to rabbits, pheasant and the trout in the local brook. Everything that I killed we ate. This was not the case for my father. The wildlife to him was mainly vermin. Crows, magpies, mink and foxes were his enemies and he was at war. He was mainly the general and would send me up to the magpie's nest at the top of tall holly bushes.

My job was to throw out the eggs or the baby birds. I remember one May evening after school. I had brought a friend up to the farm to show him around. He was a kind boy who lived in a house on the banks of the local lake. He loved to bird watch and he knew everything about every species of waterfowl, every type of fish and every creature that lived within the vantage of his bedroom window.

Now on this particular evening my father pointed out a magpie nest at the top of a tall hawthorn tree. He told me to climb up and throw down the eggs. I led my friend to the bottom of the tree and I quietly and effortlessly climbed up to the nest. There were three young chicks inside, their eyes not yet opened. When I approached and moved the nest a little they opened their mouths and cheeped, thinking that I was the parent bird arriving with food. I grabbed them and threw them down to my friend. I climbed swiftly down the tree and saw my friend. He looked to be fighting back tears. I didn't really understand why. He pointed to a chick that had been impaired on a sharp thorn of the hawthorn tree and it was wriggling around. I laughed and picked it off. I then decapitated it's head with a flick of my thumb. Mr friend did a half laugh while choking back tears. I did the same to the other two chicks and we went back to the farm. My friend excused himself and walked home.

I thought he was of inferior character. A wimp I suppose. Only now I know how much more superior a boy he was than I. He still mentions that experience from time to time and I admit to him my shame. There were mink in the vicinity of the farm, probably due to the nearby canal. They used to come to the farm on occasion and kill half a dozen hens at a time. This made my father furious. He would set snares and traps to try and catch them. One particular day I wandered into a building and I heard a real commotion. A mink was trapped in one of my father's cage traps and I knew it would not end well for it. I was older now and a lot less cold hearted towards these beautiful creatures. I tried to release it, but fear made the mink vicious and I could not get near to release the poor creature. I left to get a stick so as to release the catch from a distance. When I got back my father was there. He looked pretty pleased with himself. " I got the little bastard" he said with a smile. " I can see that" I said. I laughed and said " how are you going to get it out though? It will tear you to bits" my father said nothing, picked up the cage by the handle on the top. He then carried it to a forty five gallon drum of rain water and dropped the cage and the occupant into it. He half smiled, raised an eyebrow and walked away. It was all so pointless really. The farm is empty now. All the hens have gone, my parents dead and buried. No livestock are left in the empty fields.

I wandered up there early one morning last week. There were two deer in the field grazing the fresh green grass. Rabbits hopped around the farmyard and the rooks had made nests in the chimney. I wandered down the lane towards the canal, my mind abuz with memories, and there sulking down the hedgerow was a big dog-fox. My father was at war with the wildlife. I reckon that the wildlife won that particular battle.

Unfortunately others will come and the peace will again giveaway to the killing fields once more. I, however, changed allegiance long ago. I fight for the wildlife now, who will be strong and stand with me?

CHAPTER NINE: MENTAL HEALTH

Not so fun fact: The Health and Safety Executive has not published data on stress in farming. However, in 2019, 102 suicides by individuals working in agricultural and related trades were registered in England and Wales. This accounts for 2.2% of suicides in 2019, says the UK government website.

A sailor's storm is not like the landsmans.

The difference is in the retreat.

The old barn was my escape, a way out; a porthole to nothingness. I didn't want to know what other people thought might help me. I didn't want to know if I was looking grumpy or I was being quiet. So what if I was not present at family time. They don't understand that I don't want to be here. They would be far better off without me. And that old barn had a solid beam and an eight foot wall to one side of it. I had the rope to tie to the beam, but I didn't have the guts to do it. I was useless, I couldn't even hang myself. A pathetic coward, a loser. No wonder I have no friends. I hate this life and I want out. Every morning I would wake up and I was disappointed that I was alive. I dreaded my job and I dreaded being at home. Sleep was an escape but it was temporary and often I cold lay awake all night. It felt like I was ready depressed but instead of people trying to help me, they seemed to be frustrated with me and kept having a go at me. My life had fallen apart.

Everyone was against me, and I am a useless pathetic coward. Of course, none of this was true. My life is not much different now, but I am so happy and content. My wife and family are amazing and they always have my back. The only difference is my mental health is good and has been for years now. I thank god every day that I was a coward and didn't go through with it. I actually got has far as fixing the rope, standing on the wall in the barn with the rope around my neck. The voices told me to jump, they told me everyone would be better without me. And even if they weren't better off, it would serve them right if I did it. I sound like a spoiled brat don't I ? Unfortunately, that's not true. I was sick inside my head. The years of working on the farm had took its toll on me. I had been around death and suffering my all life. The hard work, seven days a week. The energy of oppressed and vulnerable animals had twisted and tangled with my own. I had done and seen terrible things and it had all caught up with me. I was having a breakdown. A breakdown of my own reality. I had realised that the reality that I had lived was alien to the vast majority of country that I lived in. I had the actualisation that my actions were cruel and brutal. I felt desperate and alone now. I wanted it all to end.

How many people have felt like this, desperate, hopeless and lost. They felt like that had nowhere to turn so they took their own life. They had the courage to actually go through with it. They had no idea that better times were ahead of them. My heart goes out to them and their loved ones. When you are in this place there is nothing anyone can do to get you out of it. If you have los a loved one this way, please rest assured there is nothing that you could have done. The difference between them and me is that they had the guts to do it and I don't. Remember, you can take a horse to water but you cannot make it drink.

When I was suffering with my mental health I did some awful things. I had terrible temper outbursts. I was quiet and sulky. I was violent and loud. I did things that I will forever carry shame in my hear for.

One dark September evening, around 9.30 if I remember correctly. I was out in the fields close to home. A dark cloud shrouded my heart and I slowly trudged toward home. Each step was a chore, as if I was walking through thick black tar. My mind was dull with dreadful thoughts about myself. Like I said, I had done some awful things and they weighed me down terribly. The lights from a nearby house outlined the frozen trees that stood before it. Their leaves hung low and drab as the year was drawing towards full autumn. A cold bite was in the air to remind me that the long winter stretched before me and a solitary dog barked in the not so far distance. I contemplated whether to go home, or to carry on my rambling. I was no company for the society there. They would be having a merry time without me and I would only spoil the mood for them.

I had moved out of the farm many years previous, but my parents still lived there. I decided to walk the mile across the fields and visit the old farm. I had no intention of visiting my parents. I would find no solas with them. My intention was to wander around the grounds and buildings, unseen and unheard.

I kept to the hedgerows so as to remain invisible to anyone who was out and about. I was well known around that area and I dreaded the thought of a polite conversation with s as dog walker, or someone out lamping.

The more I walked and the more I thought about my failings, by now tears were running down my cheeks. I was a pathetic sight and a shadow of the powerful creature I had once been.

I made it to the farm and sat with Sid, the black Labrador that was kennelled outside as guard dog. He knew me and made no noise at all. I sat beside him on the concrete pad that housed his kennel, and talked to him amid tears and curses.

Sid put his nose to my face and licked me, but after a while he slipped back into his kennel. He knew it was best to leave me be. I had hit the bottom with a bang, and it hurt so badly I was adamant that I could bare it no longer.

I went to the tack room where, among the harness and saddles, I kept a strong nylon, blue rope. I took the rope into the old barn and threw it up to the top of the eight foot wall which was once part of a raised boaks, that's a kind of platform to stack hay on, I climbed up silently and fastened the rope around the beam. I had recently been practicing a hangman's knot for just such an occasion. I tied one, secured the rope and placed it tightly around my neck. It felt uncomfortable and a little itchy. I remember thinking that I was so silly to think about the comfort of the rope moments before it was going to kill me. I imagined that it was going to get a lot more uncomfortable in a minute or two. This made me let out a little laugh. Just then from a small stone, ancient, air vent a white object silently floated past me and landed on a tin barrel at the far side of the barn, near the open door. By the dull light from outside I could see it was a barn owl. It looked up at me and softly flew outside.

I was surprised to see an owl in the barn. I had never seen an owl in that barn or any other barn on the farm. You will probably guess that I took this as a sign not to go through with my dreadful appointment with death. I removed the rope from around my neck and reached across to loosen the rope from the beam, but in doing so I overreached and slipped from the wall hitting the floor with a thud. I laid there for some time until any pain and shock subsided. I pulled myself to my feet and went home. I told no one about my night and climbed into bed and thought about that barn owl and what might have happened.

I would truly like to tell you that I was cured and never had those dark thoughts again, but I cannot. I continued with bouts of depression for another two years or so. However, salvation did come and it started shortly after my trip to Edinburgh. I mentioned running away to Edinburgh earlier in this book. I stoped eating meat on my return and soon after that I became vegan. Within a year I was no longer depressed and the acute eczema that had plagued me since I was a boy was completely gone. I will never be the old me, and I am thrilled to bits about it. I am, however, the happiest I can ever remember being and I never again thought about taking my life.

I never approached a doctor or psychiatrist about my mental health problems and I suffered for over ten years. I was lucky, I can so close to ending my own life. If I could give any advice, it would be to seek medical help at the first sign of depression. You will know it when you feel it. Speak to family and friends and do not bottle it up and let it grow into the monster that terrorized me.

I am cured now. I feel that becoming vegan cured me. I am not a mental health professional. So I am in no way giving medical advice. I am giving anyone who is suffering with mental health issues right now, hope. There is light at the end of the tunnel, sunshine after the storm. Please seek help, it is not hopeless. I was lucky enough to have the support of my amazing wife Louise.

CHAPTER 10: LOUISE

Reality is but a dream, and every time I wake,

I find I'm sat beside you on the banks of angel lake.

The sun was restricted by the willow tree that shaded the whole garden. Yet, beams of light cut through the leafy shield like lasers, hitting the ground and creating little, dancing stars across the lawn. There was nothing special about the choreography, nor was there anything special about the warm breeze that created it.

However, this particular day holds fast in my memory. I still remember the sound of the children playing on the nearby park. A lawnmower buzzed in the distance and the humming of the bees on the Cotoneaster that grew over the lattice fence behind me, gives the afternoon a storybook feel when I recollect it now. She walked into my life. So feminine, gentle and tender. Her voice was as soft as a newly fallen snow, but her eyes were as wild and dark as storm clouds that had plagued my heart for so long. I stared intensely at this Aphrodite as she took a turn around my humble grounds. She turned her head towards me and our eyes locked for what seemed an eternity, but must in reality, have been less than a second. My whole body melted, as I toiled to maintain composure. This vision invaded my being completely. My every unconscious thought belonged to her. She starred in every dream and cameod in my decisions.

On introspection, I usually find myself to be a little eccentric, but otherwise a sensible man, not at all given to bouts of romantic fantasies; but being somewhat of a platonist, I should have known that there was more to this chance meeting than a mere attraction. Louise was going to become a massive part of my life.

At the time I was going through a breakup with my first wife. We had both changed and even though we had changed in the same direction; the change had rendered us incompatible. Therefore we had decided to separate. The reason that Louise was taking a turn round the garden was that she was accompanied by my ex-wife because they we're friends.

As you can imagine, falling in love with your wife's best friend, no matter how cliche it might sound, is a problematic situation. I regrettably admit that I tried to fight the situation. I tried to deny myself the authenticity of my feelings, but fate it would seem, is an omniscient master and most futile to oppose.

Three difficult years passed by before Louise and I, on the road to Appleby Horse Fair, were married. The ceremony took place by the side of the river Ribble , under a rustic railway bridge on the outskirts of Clapham village.

Oh, how the winds have blown and the storms have battered our lives since then. So much so that I am sure a lesser love would have crumbled and disappeared into the emptiness of yesterday.

However, when the storms subside and the sun again shines upon us, how sweet is life and immortality would be a treasure indeed.

I have never felt such happiness nor have I ever had so much respect for another human being. Louise was vegetarian when I first met her. As I mentioned earlier in the book, After my Edinburgh trip I decided to stop eating meat.

I remember being a little worried about protein and calcium, all the misinformation given to us by the meat and dairy industry gave me a few doubts about giving up their products. However, Louise had studied nutrition for many years and gave me a chart that showed me the nutrients of meat and the vegetarian alternatives. I confidently enjoyed the vegetarian lifestyle. I am a man of a moderately muscular build and I was always quite proud of my physique. After a few months of being vegetarian I found to my great surprise that I had gained muscle, or lost body fat, so as to make my muscles more pronounced. Louise had given me a meal plan that included soy products, lentils and legumes, nuts and vegetables. I felt better in myself but I still had my bad back, knees and a swollen big toe. But at least I was not eating an animal. I knew deep down that I was still killing animals by consuming eggs and dairy and it bothered me. Louise suggested becoming vegan and I was toying with the idea. Then in 2016 we decided to watch the documentary "Cowspiracy". We both became vegan as soon as we finished watching it. Furthermore, we both got involved in animal activism.

Veganism has been the easiest transformation that I have been through. I am fitter now in middle age than I was in my 20's. I lift heavier, walk further, and last longer in everything that I do. I also no longer have the swollen toe, the bad back and knees and I no longer suffer from bouts of depression.

Louise feels the same. She now runs marathons and has got a place in the 2024 London marathon. If it wasn't for Louise, I wouldn't have become vegetarian and therefore vegan. I made a promise to my parents that I would never put them in a care home, and as old age caught up with them we had to care for them more and more. Louise would cook meals and clean their house every day.

I would shower my father a couple of times a week until he died in 2020. My mother suffered from dementia and became bed bound. My sisters couldn't accommodate her in their homes, so Louise insisted on taking her into our home. She cared for her without help for almost two years. I will never forget what Louise has done for me. Because of her I was able to keep an unrealistic promise that I made to them.

She is truly a firefly in the blackness of my twisted life.

CHAPTER 11: THE ANIMAL FARMER

The fighter fights,

The builder builds,

The farmer farms,

But the fox observes .

The animal farmer, what a familiar sight in the countryside around Britain. Usually sporting some form of headwear, overalls and green wellington boots.

They will be driving some sort of four wheel drive vehicle. In days gone by, no self respecting farmer would be seen in anything less than a Landrover Defender. Then came the Toyota Hilux. Then came the Mitsubishi L200. Then came the Nissan Navara. Then came the Ford Ranger. Now, you could find them in any of the above and many more four wheel drive vehicles. It is clear to those who know farmers, that the four wheel drive is quintessential in creating the perfect persona for the farmer. They traditionally would be towing some form of Ifor Williams livestock trailer. But even the trusty Ifor Williams can be replaced with the Nugent or the Graham Edwards and so on. My point is that even the farming community changes in some way or another.

Once the horse was the power on the farms. Then small 40/50 horsepower tractors took over. Now 200/300 horsepower tractors are commonplace.

You would see farmers walking up hill and dale with sacks of provin or bales of hay on their backs. Now they buzz around on quad bikes and variations, like angry wasps. Most farmers are born into farming. It would either be impossible or stupid to set up in animal agriculture now. The cost to buy a farm and stock it would cost a person millions of pounds with small rewards and long hours. Surly someone who could lay their hands on such riches would invest in something that would pay larger dividends than animal agriculture.

However, there was subsidies that were and still are paid to the farmers, through the government "Basic Payment Scheme". With this particular scheme, the farmer will receive around £230.00 per hectare and the average UK farm is 85 hectares. This means the farmer will receive almost £20,000 per year in subsidies. That's got to help a little. There are 216,000 farm's registered in the uk. According to defra: As per the annual report, £1.65 billion in direct subsidies were awarded to farmers in 2021/22, in line with the figures set out in the Agricultural Transition Plan. The piece reports that only 0.44% of the £2.4 bn budget was spent on the Sustainable Farming Incentive last year, 2021/22.

That's just food for thought.

Now, farming as I know it, is steeped in tradition. Most farmers marry farmers. They wouldn't marry a, "towny" unless they had a good job; may be a solicitor or someone who has a successful business. You definitely wouldn't marry a poor person, or a factory worker, or someone from a council estate.

No, I distinctly remember my mother telling my sisters that they had to marry a rich farmer's son. She was adamant that I was to marry a rich farmer's daughter.

I did marry twice, both originated from a council estate and both were better and stronger characters than I. There was a lot of snobbery in the farming when I was involved in it. I , of course, was the black sheep of our farming family.

There was also snobbery among farmers. Farmers would show their wealth by the kind of tractor they owed. A Ford or a Massey Ferguson, a Case International we're all good makes. A universal or a Zetor were the poor farmers' choice. Even now you can pass a roadside farm and see a top of the range tractor parked in a spot with a full view from the road. A farmer was judged by the acreage of his farm, many head of cattle or sheep they own and the size of their tractor. This was instilled into the minds of farmers when they were very young. I was forced to join the local "young farmer's club". My sister wanted to join, so as to meet a nice farmer's son. Unfortunately for me, she didn't want to go on her own. My parents forced me, at the age of eleven, to go with her.

In the summer months the male club members would do activities like judging cows, or tractor handling; while the girls would learn how to bake buns or flower arrangement. Women were expected to cook and clean, while the men worked the land and took care of the animals. I was speaking to an old acquaintance who is a young farmers club leader. I asked him if this still happened at the clubs and he said that it definitely does not. Equality has found the young farmers!

There was a lot of strutting about bragging about new tractors, or new buildings that had been erected on their farms when I was a member . I didn't really fit in there and never enjoyed it much. I had to continue until my sister had made a decent friend group and then I stopped going.

I know that I have mentioned this before, but it is important to understand that animal agriculture is a business and that the animals are assets. In farming, even today, the profit is tight. Even tighter than it was 20 years ago. There is no room for sentiment. This is true in every business. It just so happens that farmers deal in live animals, just like an electrician deals with electricity and it's components. In business there is no place for sentimental, mates rates. Business is business and that's how the world works.

Farming is supply and demand, and ther is still plenty of demand for meat and dairy products. This means that animals are still being abused. Cut the demand and you will cut the supply and so cut the amount of farm animal cruelty. This is the sad truth, as long as animals are farmed for food, then animals will be mistreated. The Animal Farmers are business people not monsters . There is no room for sentiment in business.

If you don't like this fact then don't blame the supplier, blame the consumer. If you consume animal products, blame yourself. This is my experience as an animal farmer. Women in farming are common-place nowadays. They are just as shrewd in business as the men folk and, from my experience, are just as equipped to carry out the day to day running off a busy, animal farming outfit.

Gone are the days of baking and flower arrangements. Gone are the days of the portly farmer's wife wobbling down the fields with a tray of sandwiches and bottles of pale ale for the working men in the harvest fields.

She can milk cows, shear sheep, muck-out the pigs and handle heavy plant equipment like a man and in most cases better than them. You will have seen them buzzing past you as you walk the country lanes in the Dales. You will have to look sharp though, they can be often difficult to distinguish from the males, with their ruddy red faces, wooly bobble hats, oversized fluorescent green jackets and of course, the green wellington boots.

Be warned though, stray off that public footpath and that woman is more vicious than any three males; and the language she curses in your direction is worse than any that you will hear on the many council estates around Manchester. Yet, her soul is safe. She is the chief administrator at the village church; and sometimes, just sometimes, she rings the bells when old Billy is having a senior moment and can't make the Sunday morning session. Blessed are these women, for they will inherit the farm when their husband passes to that great animal farm in the sky.

Please do not misunderstand me. I am not telling you that there are no good looking farmer's wives, there most certainly are. You will see them driving briskly down the farm track in their Range Rover sport. Their long blond hair tied back in a ponytail by the way of a black scrunchy. A new layer of mid pink lipstick applied to their moist lips as they speeds along to the local court room to defend her husband's mother's cousin, four times removed, who faces charges of kidnapping a young backpacker who wandered off the footpath. However, in reality it was the defendant's sister who actually kidnapped the girl, but her brother has taken the heat, so as to help his sister save face with Mr Palmer the local vicar and all at St Mary's. The last part of the above is not true, it's a bit of imagination designed to bring a little humor to, what up to now, has been quite an dismal read. Although, my cousin Sandra, if asked, would have at least two tales of local Ingelton farmers that would match the above story. And her son, Tommy, has probably written and performed a damn good thrash metal ballad about it. So I say to you, when rambling the countryside. Stick to the roads, don't worry about the full moon, it's the sound of the quad bike that you should be worried about!

Some interesting facts

• According to Statista, There are 1.85 million dairy cows in the uk and 9.4 million in the US. The total work wide dairy industry has 270 million head of cattle.

• According to www.iwto.org, Starista and government websites, there are 33 million sheep in the UK, 5.2 million sheep in the

US and 1,266 billion sheep world wide and this number is till growing. The largest sheep industries are in India and Australia, both countries recording over 2% growth in 2021/22.

• According to Statista, there are 124 million broiler chickens in the UK. Broiler chickens are used in the meat industry. According to DEFRA, there are 37 million commercial laying hens in the UK in 2023. That is down from 40 million in 21/22. 1.6 million of these hens are still caged.

• According to Statista, the UK beef industry is worth 4.4 billion pounds per annum. The

US beef industry is worth 1.226 billion dollars and is growing by 4.58% annually.

• According to Statista, there are 5.2 million pigs in the UK. There are 72.5 million in the US and 72.5 million in the commercial market worldwide. According to the RSPCA, the majority of pigs are killed by gas-stunning. This involves using high concentrations of gas mixtures, currently carbon dioxide.

•According to Viva, gassing the pigs causes them agony as the Carbon Dioxide forms acid in the pig's eyes, nostrils, mouth and lungs.

• According to the Commons library, horse meat can be prepared and sold in the UK if it meets the general requirements for selling and labeling meat. There are three abattoirs operating in the UK that are licensed to slaughter horses for human consumption. It is also legal to export live horses from the UK for slaughter if they have the necessary paperwork such as a horse passport, export license and health certification. However, this is not usual practice.

• According to Sentiment Media, the worldwide vegan food

market grew from \$14.44 billion in 2020 to \$15.77 billion in 2021 and is forecast to continue growing for the next several years. The expected growth in the vegan food industry is due to an increasing number of people seeking to reduce how much meat they eat. Vegans and nonvegans alike are seeking to replace animal-based foods with vegan ones.

The owner of a fish and chip shop once asked me, "What do you vegans think will happen to all the animals and land, if suddenly, tomorrow everyone changed to a vegan diet ?". This is the most stupid and irrelevant question that I have been asked since I became vegan. It's worse than, where do you get your protein? It's worse than where do you get your calcium? I didn't answer the man's question, as I thought it not worthy of an answer.

In reality, veganism will grow slowly. As veganism grows the demand for meat and dairy products will fall. As animal agriculture is a supply on demand industry, when the demand falls the farmers will need less animals to feed the demand and so breed less animals. Over the years as the percentage of vegans grows, the animal numbers should decline by roughly the same percentage. The land will have different uses. We will probably need more vegetables, so some land will be used for that. My guess is that more trees will be planted. The government is already giving farmers and landowners financial incentives to plant trees on their land. I would also hope that there will still be all the breeds of farm animals out there, just in smaller numbers. Living a free life without murder and abuse. I cannot accurately predict the future for farm animals. However, the world is changing , but the he changes are slow. This is because the world is presently set up to benefit the world leaders. I don't necessarily mean the prime ministers and presidents of the world. I mean the business leaders of the world, so if the world is beneficial for these world leaders; then why would the promote change? If you look at history, it's the people on the front line, the little people who start the change.

The suffragettes of the 20th century were the most unlikely group of activists to bring change. However, the world leaders slowly started to see the advantages of women having more power and so relatively quickly that change was taken on board. On the other hand, the abolition of slavery was slower, much slower. The powers thought that is slavery was abolished the financial economy would crumble. That is why the abolition movement took over a hundred years to get results. Vegans have to keep moving forward and increasing in number, then one day we will have a vegan-normal world. After that we might have a vegan only world.

CONCLUSION

In the end the rooks will feed, and the servant will become the master.

The sword and shield, decayed by rust, lies lost in lonely fields.

I will leave this old farm now. I bid farewell to its old oak beamed ceilings and its ancient stone steps.

I see and feel the ghosts that haunt this dismal place.

For what is a ghost but a forgotten memory, left behind for others to sense and feel. I can see that you are all standing with me. I feel your sorrow from what you have seen. Take warning my friends, this is no place to linger. Take from it what you need and move on. There are darker secrets here.

Yet, from the very first breath that I took in this world, there has been hope. Not Hope for me, but hope for the emancipation of farm animals. Hope of a kinder world. Human nature is often malignant and not only to animals. The atrocities inflicted by humans to humans are constant throughout history and now is no exception. In reality we have only just abolished slavery. It is relatively new for the human race not to use slave labour. Unfortunately, according to the "End Slavery Now" movement, even today there are millions of humans still trapped in some form of slavery. This is discouraging news indeed, but thanks to this movement and the individuals who every day make it their business to expose slavery, it is getting slightly lower. It is a matter of time before it is gone forever.

Animal cruelty is still in full swing all over the world. If history has taught us anything, it will take hundreds, if not thousands, of years to wipe it out. But it starts with you, right here, right now, to do something to raise awareness to the abominations of cruelty committed to farm animals worldwide every second of every day. It is a massive task and it has been appointed to us. We won't receive recognition for it ever in our lifetime. We don't need recognition . We need to do something to help, and know this if you must, that you are one of an army of heroes who will not yield until all animals are free.

One cold January morning, I met a random stranger as I walked down a country lane with Violet, a cocker spaniel. We conversed about the weather and about the dogs that accompanied us. I mentioned that I was vegan. The gentleman looked a little uncomfortable, almost disapproving in his manor. His body language changed towards me and he asked why I am vegan. I replied, "for the animals". He looked antagonised at this, and he informed me that animals eat animals. He said that you wouldn't catch a lion eating a salad sandwich. I am not sure if this is true. I would really have to take a salad sandwich to a lion and try it out. Unfortunately the only place I would find a lion at short notice would be at a zoo, and taking into consideration the fact that I think zoos are cruel prisons for animals, I wouldn't patronise one.

Now, I was never described as a scroller at school. I dare say that I have forgotten more than I remember academically. However, my old headmaster at primary school sprung to mind and his wisdom mustered a response. "If that lion jumped into the canal, would you?" I asked. The gentleman looked deep into my eyes, shook his head very slightly and walked away with his dog. Guess that I won that one!

The old stone steps at the farm had dints worn into them. They wasn't erected that way. The dints were worn over hundreds of years of people walking up and down them. In the same way animal abuse won't stop tomorrow. It will take hundreds of years of activism and campaigning before it is stopped.

We don't need to eat meat or drink milk. We don't need to wear animal skins or abuse them in the name of medical science. We are choosing to do these things because we like them. All you need to do is choose not to; then you have played your part in changing human history forever. I will end with a verse from the New Testament: Corinthians 13:4–8a (ESV) Love is patient and kind; love does not envy or boast; it is not arrogant or rude. It does not insist on its own way; it is not irritable or resentful; it does not rejoice at wrongdoing, but rejoices with the truth. I will add, it doesn't kill or saluter, it doesn't devour its devotees, it doesn't rape, it doesn't enslave or abuse.

Remember this the next time you tell someone that you love animals.

Before the stones are cast and judgements are made; remember this. If you have ever eaten meat or drank milk or worn the skin of another; you did these things with me. You stood by my side as my allies. My sins are your sins.

If it wasn't for you none of this would have happened.

You are me, if you want to be a better person, be one.

Stop abusing all animals. Stop consuming animal products.

Becoming vegan has proved to have many advantages for me. From being a young boy I had severe eczema. It came in bouts every few months but it was nearly always present on some part of my body. I think that it must be the lactose in dairy products. When I was just vegetarian it never left me, but only a few months after becoming fully vegan it started clearing up. Within six months it was fully gone.

I was diagnosed with gout by my local doctor. I had a painful swollen big toe on my left foot. Again, this would come in bouts. When I had a flare up my toe would swell and it was really painful to touch. For some reason it would wake me up at exactly 2am and hurt and ache for hours. I would have to put an ice pack on it to release the pain. I had had these symptoms for five years before going vegan, but within two months of going vegan it was gone. I had knee and back pain constantly, but again I would have bouts when the pain was severe. This generally coincided with the gout. I haven had any symptoms for almost a decade. However, the biggest life changer for me is that I no longer suffer from depression. I no longer have that terrible temper and I don't overreact to testing situations.

I know that I have done some terrible things in my life, but I forgive myself. I made a pact with God, that never again will I do cruel or abusive things to people or animals. That I will treat others how I would like to be treated myself. I will never again be a hard unforgiving human being. I know that somewhere deep inside me that cold hearted hard and vicious person lays dormant. But I choose to be kind to my fellow man. And instead of being an animal abuser, I will be forever an animal defender.